A Good Friend for Bad Times

Helping Others through Grief

DISCARD

Deborah E. Bowen and Susan L. Strickler

Augsburg Books
MINNEAPOLIS

A GOOD FRIEND FOR BAD TIMES
Helping Others through Grief

Large-quantity purchases or custom editions of this book are available at a
discount from the publisher. For more information, contact the sales department at Augsburg Fortress, Publishers, P. O. Box 1209, Minneapolis, MN
55440-1209.

Cover design by Marti Naughton, photo © Phil Leo/Getty Images
Book design by Michelle L. N. Cook, author photos by Dennis S. Reifsnider

Library of Congress Cataloging-in-Publication Data
Bowen, Deborah E., 1951-
  A good friend for bad times : helping others through grief / Deborah E.
Bowen, Susan L. Strickler.
       p. cm.
  Includes bibliographical references.
  ISBN 0-8066-5151-2 (alk. paper)
  1. Grief. 2. Bereavement—Psychological aspects. 3. Death—Psychological
aspects. 4. Consolation. I. Strickler, Susan L., 1945- II. Title.
  BF575.G7B677 2004
  155.9'37—dc22   2004008226

The paper used in this publication meets the minimum requirements of
American National Standard for Information Sciences—Permanence of Paper
for Printed Library Materials, ANSI Z329.48-1985. ⊛ ™

Special note: In the examples used in this book, all names have been changed,
as have some of the details of the cases, to protect client/friend confidentiality.

Manufactured in the U.S.A.

08   07   06   05   04   1   2   3   4   5   6   7   8   9   10

In loving memory of our parents
Warren Brooks Bowen and Mary Kathryn Horne Bowen
and Barbara Tunison Lamson and Edward Nathan Lamson
and of Merlin, the Magic Cat

In love and honor of
Tracy B. Martin, Greg Martin, Travis Martin, and Stuart Martin
and Herbert Randolph Strickler, Brooks Walton Strickler,
Carla Strickler, and Nathan Randall Strickler

For all their loving support

Contents

Acknowledgments   vii
1. Understanding the Grieving Process   1
2. Anticipatory Grief   11
3. Between Death and the Ceremony   23
4. The Ceremony and Immediately After   35
5. The First Weeks after Death   45
6. The First Month and Up to a Year after Death: 57
   Providing Emotional Support for Your Friend
7. The First Month and Up to a Year after Death: 69
   Providing Physical Support for Your Friend
8. Special Considerations   81
9. Holidays and Special Events   95
10. Death by Catastrophe   105
11. Supporting Children through Grief   115
Conclusion   121
Notes   123
Selected Bibliography   125
Internet Resources   129
About the Authors   131

Acknowledgments

We both extend heartfelt thanks to our clients and friends who shared their burden of grief with us. We thank the board of directors and staff of Lower Cape Fear Hospice and LifeCareCenter, Wilmington, North Carolina, for their encouragement and support. We particularly thank Ellen Cameron, MSW, LCSW, without whom this book would not have happened, and Nan Chandler, MSW, LCSW, for her assistance with the section about children. Finally, there are not enough words to express our gratitude to our agent, Alice McElhinney, and to our editors, Lois Wallentine and Eric Vollen.

I, Deb, wish to thank the following people: Joyce Cooper for her editorial comments, humor, and unwavering faith in my writing skills; the Delta Training Partners, Inc. boys—Kevin Coughlin,

Sam Lewis, Dave Smith, and Charlie Coulter—for teaching me to write; and Roselle Margolis for valuable information regarding Jewish traditions. A special word of appreciation is extended to Gail Dubov for reviewing the initial manuscript, urging me to pursue the project, and offering valuable publishing information.

My family suffered such loss when my parents died, and I am grateful to so many relatives: Clayton (in memoriam) and Jo Ann Horne and their family, Norman and Mildred Miller (in memoriam) and their family, Shirley and Ken Buie and their family, James and Joyce Bowen (in memoriam) and their family.

Special thanks to my dear friends who have shared grief over so many losses with me: John and Carol Bates, Andrea Burgess, Dawn Carmen Casey and John Casey, Gene and Billie Carmen, Ralph Davis and Jean Sloop-Davis, Raven Davis, Jeanne Denny, Ann Foltrauer, Jon Guttman (in memoriam), Joel Hawkins, Don and Wanda Johnson, Angie Olson King, Dottie Lamb, Sue Lamb, Nicki Leone, Ginny Lundeen, Ken McCracken, Laura McLean, Sue Naset, Janet Parsons, Paul Parsons, Kimberly Paul, Adriana Pridgen, Nancy Ramsaur, Jeff Reid, Randall and Diane Smith, Jane Spellman, Terri-Lynn Sykes, Pat Thibedeaux, Robin Tickner, White Eagle and Thunder Dove, and Drew Wyatt.

Deep gratitude is extended to my sister's friends (who have become mine as well) who cared for me so tenderly when my parents died: Danielle and Bobby Ahouse, Linda and Bobby Canaday, Sheila and Roger Foxworth, Terri and Mac Hall, Robin and Wayne Lanier, Cathy Leonard, Jeanne and David Plowden, Patti and Lynn Raynor, D'Arcy and Hunter Smith, Linda and Kirby Smith, Carolyn and Eujay Thibodeaux, and Janice and Rudy Webb.

Many thanks to my parents' friends, and to the members of the congregation of their church, Blake's Chapel Advent Christian Church, Sloop Point, North Carolina. Heartfelt thanks is extended to the staff of Cornelia Nixon Davis Health Care Center, Wilmington, North Carolina, for the tenderness shown to my mother.

Appreciation is extended to my professional colleagues and friends: faculty and staff of the University of North Carolina at Wilmington Department of Social Work and Center for Leadership Education and Service, East Carolina University School of Social Work, and members of the board of directors of the National Association of Social Workers, North Carolina chapter.

I, Sue, extend my thanks to all those whose aid and support made this book possible. I am grateful to my colleagues at Lower Cape Fear Hospice and LifeCareCenter. Their dedication and capacity for care make them special to all those who receive their loving care. A thank you also goes to Laurie Myles, executive director of Lower Cape Fear Hospice and LifeCareCenter for her support and confidence in my work. I would also like to acknowledge Jane Barefoot who hired me many years ago. She has been a mentor and inspiration over the years. Last, but not least, I express my deep gratitude to my clients who have shared their grief with me and taught me so much. They certainly have been my finest teachers.

Chapter 1

Understanding
the Grieving Process

Your coworker's husband dies after a long illness. Should you send flowers? Your neighbor suffers a miscarriage. Should you cook dinner and take it to her? An old friend's mother dies, and seven months later he still declines your invitations to play golf. Should you stop calling? We ask ourselves these questions, and many others, when friends and coworkers suffer loss. We are often unsure what to do or say, because we fear we will do or say something wrong. This book contains suggestions about what to do or not to do, and what to say or not to say, when someone you know grieves.

Much of the information in this book was gleaned from our own experiences with loss. We are orphans. Both of us have lost both our parents; most recently, our mothers. We also are professional mental-health practitioners who specialize in caretaker and grief issues. We are well versed in the scholarly literature on grief, loss, death, and dying. When we suffered our own losses, however, we realized that all the theories, all the storehouses of knowledge, and all the tales of others' experiences did not prepare us completely for coping with our own grief.

We have worked for years with grieving clients who have suffered many different kinds of losses, including deaths of a spouse, a parent, a child, a fiancé, a pet. We have helped people cope with miscarriages and abortions. We also know people who grieve losses other than death: a move from a beloved home or city, destroyed property from natural disasters, or loss of mobility due to illness. The notion of "secondary losses" can also be brought about by happy events, such as marriage, retirement, or a career change. During these times people may experience feelings of sadness, confusion, or fear, and they may wonder why they are not happy at such a joyous time in their lives. Many grieve more than one loss at any one given time. This is called "compounded grieving."

Our clients have taught us a tremendous amount about their grieving processes, about their individual circumstances, and their methods of coping with loss. We are immeasurably grateful to them, and humbled by their willingness to share their stories and pain with us.

We learned in our own grieving experiences and, from our clients, that the best support and comfort came from our families, friends, coworkers, and spiritual leaders. We learned that while grief is intensely personal and individual, we could not grieve in a vacuum. We needed the help of many others to make our way through the morass of pain.

We have discovered, however, that many friends and coworkers do not have the tools to assist someone who is grieving. Well-intentioned questions or comments cut like knives. "When will you be back to normal?" "You need to get on with your life." "You can't cry forever." Yet, in fact, there were times when we did not want to carry on with our lives, when we believed we could, or would, cry forever.

While there are many models of how we grieve, brief overviews of three of the most well known and accepted are presented later in this chapter. None of these models, however, takes into account cultural and historical differences in the grieving process; nor do they take into account the rapid changes in support systems and society today. For example, during the 1800s in the United States, a woman typically wore black for a year after the death of her husband, and she was governed by strict etiquette concerning her behavior during that year. Usually, her family lived close by and made sure that she was cared for during that mourning period. Today, families are scattered across the globe, and many of us do not know our neighbor's name. Most employers provide three days of "funeral leave" in the event of a death in the family. After those three days, an employee is supposed to "be back to normal." The truth is, grief does not work that way.

Grieving happens the way it happens. There are no rights or wrongs. Each of us grieves in his own way, in his own time. Certainly, there are similarities among us in the range of our emotions and actions, but circumstances for each of us are unique.

There are literally thousands of books about grief and bereavement, many of them excellent resources for the grieving person. However, we have found very few that provide clear, concise information for those of us who support friends, family members, and coworkers during and after times of loss. This book was written to support the supporters.

Understanding the Grieving Process

Most Americans today have at least some familiarity with the most widely known of the grieving models, so this section is intended as a brief overview. Please refer to the suggested reading list in the back of this book for more information.

One of our clients, Sally, told us that she was "numb" for the first year after her father died. She said, "It was as if I were holding on to a fraying rope by my toenails until the anniversary date of his death, trying to do all the 'right' things to settle his estate. It wasn't until after the estate was settled, and he'd been dead over a year, that I allowed myself to really cry."

Another client, Bob, told us that he left his mother's hospital room for "just five minutes," and when he returned, she was dead. He said he vomited on the hospital room floor, and continued to vomit several times over the course of three days.

What is grief? *Webster's New World Dictionary* defines the word *grief* as "intense emotional suffering caused by loss." *Bereave* is defined as "to leave in a sad or lonely state, as in death." *Mourning* is defined as "a sorrowing; specifically the expression of grief at someone's death." Therefore, mourning is the outward display of grieving emotions caused by being bereft of someone or something. Mourning is also a cultural response to grief. There is no one style of grief. Grief is a reaction that is socially and culturally influenced.

Many theories attempt to explain how we grieve, to describe the emotions of grief, and what expected actions are during the grieving process. Most of these theories have merit, but three of them are the most widely known and widely accepted models that describe the grieving process. The models discussed in this section state that a person generally needs at least a year to work through the emotions of grief and to commemorate important anniversary dates. The models state that some people never finish grieving and that grieving emotions are not sequential, so that the stages noted below may not be in any particular order. In addition, several emotions may occur simultaneously, with one emotion sometimes masking another.

The Westberg Model

Granger Westberg, in his 1962 landmark book *Good Grief,* noted ten stages in the grieving process.[1]

1. *Shock and denial.* Bob, the client mentioned above, went into shock upon the death of his mother. The vomiting was a symptom of that shock. Another client, Ann, said, "I held my

husband's hand while he was dying and, after he breathed his last breath, I couldn't let go. I believed if I held on to his body, he couldn't die." Barbara said that she became "a zombie," unable to think about anything immediately after the death of her mother. "My husband, bless him, splashed cold water in my face to bring me out of shock." Jean just kept repeating, "No! No! This is just a bad dream!" when learning of her daughter's death.

Shock and initial denial occur as the mind's way of protecting us from the impact of tragic loss. Often, we act as if nothing is out of the ordinary; our brains simply cannot process the intense pain. Again, while there are no time limits, for some people this stage is experienced for a few minutes; for others, hours or days. According to individual circumstances, each person experiences these emotions differently.

2. *Emotions erupt.* Crying, screaming, or sighing usually marks this stage. One of the saddest sights Deb has ever seen was an adult friend pounding on a hospital room floor, screaming, "I want my daddy! I want my daddy!" about ten minutes after his father died.

Often, immediately after death, shock, denial, and crying alternate in rapid succession. Bob said that during the three days before his mother's funeral, he chatted with friends about the stock market, burst into tears upon seeing roses, and threw up repeatedly.

3. *Anger.* Claire's sister had suffered for a long time with a terminal illness. When Claire was told her sister had only a matter of hours to live, she called her sister's minister, asking him to come to the hospital. Generally, over the course of her sister's illness, the minister had been supportive to the family. However, his response was less than supportive: "We have prayer meeting tonight, and we will pray for her." Claire screamed at the minister, "Doesn't your Bible have that story in it about leaving the ninety-nine sheep while you search for the lost one? I'm losing my sister! What kind of Christian minister are you?"

Anger can be directed at anyone, any time, and for no apparent reason. Sometimes we are angry with God (or whatever we perceive as a higher power) or a representative of spirituality, as in Claire's case. Sometimes we are angry with the person who dies, feeling deserted and abandoned. Sometimes we take out our frustration on other loved ones, medical professionals, or the person driving the car in front of us.

4. *Illness.* Because grief is stressful, stress-related illnesses often occur during the grieving process. Helen lost both her parents in a car crash several years ago. About four months after they died, she developed shingles, a painful form of herpes that is caused by stress. Colds, flu, gastrointestinal ailments, tension headaches, ulcers, and hypertension are common after loss.

5. *Panic.* Unfamiliar emotions may surface during the grieving process or familiar emotions may appear in a new intensity. Nightmares, hyperventilation, and seemingly uncontrollable illnesses may send us into panic. Panic is often manifested by additional hyperventilation, racing heartbeats, sweating, and an inability to think clearly. A client who was grieving the loss of an older brother had repeated panic attacks during the first few months after the death, and believed he was having heart attacks. Fortunately, the client had a good physician who recognized his grief symptoms.

6. *Guilt.* We call this stage the "if only" stage. "If only I had or had not . . ." We humans do not like to be out of control, to feel powerless. We are uncomfortable with feelings of helplessness. Westberg says that this stage of self-blame is universal. Family members often refuse to leave the dying person's bedside for even a minute, believing that as long as they stay, the dying person will not die. Hospice workers say that, in fact, this often is the case, as if the dying person does not want to die in front of someone.

7. *Depression and loneliness.* Overwhelming sadness and feelings of isolation occur frequently in the grieving process. Sometimes folks withdraw from friends and family, cry, and think about only negative events and feelings. This is the most commonly recognized and accepted grief stage, and will be discussed in detail later.

8. *Reentry difficulties.* For almost a year after her husband died, Margaret cried every morning while brushing her teeth. She refused to part with her husband's toothbrush or any of his belongings. Friends invited her to attend symphony performances, something she had said for years she was going to do when she had time, but she refused. Slowly, she began to accept invitations. During this stage, says Westberg, the grieving person tries to build a new life for herself.

9. *Hope.* Westberg says that hope returns gradually and that putting one's life back together can happen.

10. *Affirming reality.* In this stage, the person puts his life back together, although it is different than it was before the loss. Memories certainly remain, but the new life is satisfactory.

Westberg, as noted, states that there is considerable movement back and forth among the stages, but that stages nine and ten are not generally reached until one has had ample time to work through the other eight stages. He also states that some people never successfully reach the last two stages but spend the rest of their lives in the other eight stages. Later in this book we will discuss situations in which this event is most likely to occur.

The Kübler-Ross Model

Elisabeth Kübler-Ross's landmark book, *On Death and Dying,* was first published in 1969.[2] In this book, the psychiatrist identified a range of emotions experienced by people who were *dying.* Yet over time, her theory was used to describe the experience of those *grieving* a death or other types of loss. It should be noted that many experts on grief criticize Kübler-Ross's study, as her subjects were all volunteers. They believe her methodology was flawed and her results were misinterpreted and wrongly applied to the experience of grieving. Yet her work opened the door for providing psychological counseling to the dying and paved the way for people to talk about death, dying, and grieving issues.

While Kübler-Ross's model is similar to Westberg's, she has simplified the process and incorporated some of Westberg's stages into some of her stages. She, like Westberg, notes that her stages are not sequential, and that there is considerable movement back and forth among the stages. She agrees with Westberg that at least a year must pass before grieving can be complete.

1. *Denial.* This stage helps cushion the emotional impact of the event. "This can't be happening" is one familiar comment heard during this stage. Carl, upon being told by the doctor that his wife had pneumonia and had just a few days to live, responded with, "Oh, thank goodness! She's had pneumonia many times. She'll get through this bout and go home." There also is an element of shock in this stage, at least initially, after a loss. After his son died, Mark refused to leave the body, continuing to speak to his child's body as if he were not dead.

2. *Rage and anger.* Kübler-Ross's anger stage is very much like Westberg's in that God, the dying or dead person, the medical professionals, and others are often the target of the grieving person's anger.

3. *Bargaining.* This stage is often exhibited before a loved one dies. Many times bargains are attempted with God, and they sometimes seem to work. Don's physician told him to expect to live only a few weeks after he was diagnosed with cancer. He explained to the doctor that he had to live until he walked his daughter down the aisle at her wedding, some five months away. Although he was pushed in a wheelchair, he did indeed walk her down the aisle and then died a few days later.

4. *Depression/despair.* This stage, like Westberg's, exhibits a hopelessness and often overwhelming sadness. This is a normal part of the grief process, and the painful time when one really understands that the death has occurred. This is a time when one feels life is meaningless. There is little motivation and energy. "Nothing means anything to me anymore" and "I feel like a part of me died with him" are commonly heard.

5. *Acceptance.* Kübler-Ross says that in this stage, the loss is acknowledged and survivors learn to cope and begin to look for alternatives for their lives.

Some experts strongly warn against thinking of grief as requiring a "recovery process." They urge people not to use Kübler-Ross's model as a litmus test with which to judge a griever's progress toward being "over" a death or loss. Every person's experience with grief is different. "You are grieving your loss in a 'get-over-it,' 'move-on-with-it' world," says Dr. Harold Ivan Smith, a certified death, dying, and bereavement counselor and author of many books on grief. "After a death, there is no getting back to 'normal.' Over time, if you cooperate with grief, a new 'normal' emerges. The process of grieving is never finished, although our culture does its best to rush grievers through their grief."[3]

The Worden Model

J. William Worden's *Grief Counseling and Grief Therapy: A Handbook for the Mental Health Practitioner* is the primary source used by hospice bereavement professionals in working with people who are grieving.[4] He outlines four tasks of mourning in this work.

1. *To accept the reality of the loss.* In this stage, there is a sense of denial, shock, and numbness. There is a strong feeling that the death has not happened. The goal of this task is to fully face the fact that the person is dead and will not return.

2. *To work through to the pain of the loss.* This time can be characterized by crying, nausea, loss of appetite, irritability, physical illness symptoms, fear, and preoccupation with the deceased. This task is focused on the emotional and psychological acceptance of the loss. Loneliness, depression, guilt, and anger may occur. During this period, the grieving person needs to deal with any unfinished business he may have had with the dead person. The goal of this task is to experience the pain of loss so that the pain can diminish some over time.

3. *To adjust to environments in which the person is missing.* During this time, the grieving person adapts to life without her loved one. The survivor becomes aware of the roles played by the deceased person and may feel disoriented as she begins to reorganize her life. She may feel helpless and inadequate, and she may feel some resentment about having to develop new skills. The grieving person needs to adjust to both new and old situations without the deceased. The goal of this task is to face the situations in which the deceased is especially missed, rather than avoiding these experiences. Grievers will also begin to reconnect with a sense of the future.

4. *To "relocate" and memorialize the life.* For many people, this is the most difficult task. People often remain in this period for a long time, putting all of their energy into focusing on the loss. The goal of this task is to accept the loss, to find a way to remember the deceased, and to begin rebuilding one's life. The survivor starts to reach out to form new relationships, or strengthen old ones, and to begin a life without the deceased.

In our work, we have found that one emotion often masks another, particularly when the grieving person perceives that a given emotion is not considered acceptable. For example, in some cultures women are not allowed to express anger. Consequently, anger often appears as depression. Conversely, in some cultures, men are not allowed to cry, so they appear angry. Recognizing the real emotion is sometimes difficult, both for the grieving person and for his support system.

An awareness of the stages of grief does not change the emotions of grief. A survivor can cognitively understand that she is experiencing depression, for example, but that knowledge does not change or take away the depression. It is imperative that those of us who support a grieving person can recognize the underlying emotion and offer appropriate support.

The remaining chapters of this book offer clear, concise ways of offering that support, beginning well before death and continuing for at least a year afterward.

Chapter 2

Anticipatory Grief

Experiencing the cycle of grief emotions prior to loss is called anticipatory grieving. As mentioned in chapter 1, sometimes we deny the diagnosis; we are certain someone read the wrong X ray or test. We are depressed about the changes in our loved one's bodily functioning and appearance. We are saddened by thoughts of future life events that will not be shared. We bargain for time to enjoy a future deadline: children's graduations, the birth of a grandchild, a favorite holiday. We are angry at the prospect of leaving too soon; we rage against the inadequacies and ineptitude of the medical profession; we think we have mistakenly trusted in a higher power who cannot perform miracles.

If the grieving cycle is allowed to complete itself, there comes a time when the dying person and his family and friends reach a level of acceptance. This is not to say we like or understand the inevitable outcome, but we are resigned to death. Hopefully, during this period, the dying person and his loved ones experience a sense of peace.

Just as in grief after loss, there are no rules about how one grieves in anticipation of a loss. Certain words automatically trigger a grieving response: cancer, HIV, AIDS, heart attack, stroke. This is true even when the patient lives for many years with the illness or apparently recovers (as in the case of heart attack). In these situations, there seems to be a death sentence hanging over the patient and his family.

Gail was diagnosed with ovarian cancer at age forty-six. She, her husband, parents, and two daughters, ages twenty and twenty-four, initially faced the diagnosis with shock, denial, and tears. From the first minute after they were told the prognosis, they began the process of anticipatory grieving. Anticipatory grieving occurs before the physical loss actually happens. It appears much like grieving after a loss, including the same stages described by Westberg, Kübler-Ross, and Worden.

Gail and her family had a large extended family and many friends. She called her closest friends and family members, asking them to come to her home on the Sunday after her doctor explained his proposed course of treatment. More than twenty friends and family members gathered at Gail's home.

Gail and her husband explained the illness and its prognosis to them. They asked for support, both physical and emotional. "Who can help around the house, particularly while I'm in the hospital? The dog needs to be fed, the plants need to be watered, the grass needs to be mowed, the laundry needs to be done, the cars need to be maintained, and the bills need to be paid on time. We need you to tell us that you love us and that you'll pray for us." Tasks were chosen by those who were willing to undertake them and, as Gail's husband described it, "the siege began."

Does this story seem unrealistic to you? Who, in the face of such a crisis, would have the forethought to make such arrangements? While this situation is indeed true, it is unusual. Most people face those first few moments or days after such a diagnosis with shock and denial. People do not always know what they need—both physically and emotionally—or how to ask for help.

Indeed, Gail and her family did experience feelings of unreality and helplessness, and all the other emotions described by Westberg, Kübler-Ross, and Worden during the months preceding her death. However, planning and asking for support played a crucial role in making Gail's last months more comfortable, and in allowing her family more quality time with her.

Anticipatory grieving can go on for years. Bill, a powerful executive in a law firm, had no plans for retirement. He worked every day and golfed and fished with old friends on weekends. He was devoted to his wife, Sarah, their son and daughter, and their grandchildren. When Bill was sixty-three, Sarah began to notice subtle changes in his speech and behavior. He forgot where he put his keys; he mixed up the names of his grandchildren. Normally quite placid at home, he now became irritated by small household upsets. Sarah attributed his forgetfulness to old age, shrugged off the episodes, and covered up his strange comments and behavior in front of others.

At the family gathering for his sixty-fourth birthday, his children presented him with a new set of golf clubs. After unwrapping the box, he stared blankly at the clubs, and said very seriously, "These will catch lots of fish." His family sat in stunned silence. At last, they could no longer deny that something was radically wrong. A battery of tests indicated that Bill was in the early stages of Alzheimer's disease.

Bill and his family lived for twelve years with this illness. For the first four years, Sarah kept Bill at home. As the disease progressed, Bill began to wander away from home and became increasingly combative. It became more and more difficult to care for Bill. Against his wishes, Sarah placed him in a long-term care facility designed especially for people with memory impairment illnesses.

Bill's family experienced anticipatory grief, but for a long time. In addition to the grief stages mentioned earlier, Bill's family also felt guilt about placing Bill in a facility, and had reentry difficulties after Bill left home. Suddenly, Sarah found herself with time to go out to dinner with friends or to just watch television without being hypervigilant about Bill's behaviors. While she was relieved that Bill was safe and well cared for, she felt guilty about going on with her life and visited him daily.

In both of the scenarios presented here, the families had time to grieve and prepare for the eventual outcome. However, it cannot be assumed that because a death is anticipated, those grieving the upcoming loss are prepared for death. Some people do not take this opportunity to say good-bye or to express their emotions for the dying person. They may be in denial or feel uncomfortable saying good-bye. Too often, we think like this person: "I can't give up. If I talk to Roger about his dying and my feelings of helplessness and fear, he will give up too."

Is there a difference when the anticipation period is dramatically shorter than mentioned in the two scenarios above? For example, what is the family's grieving process when a child lives only a few days after birth? What might be expected for a family when a teenager is brought unconscious to the hospital after a car accident? What if there is no opportunity to say good-bye, or to know for sure that your farewell had been heard by the dying person? With little advance notice of the impending death, there may be no time for anticipatory grief. The timetable for experiencing various emotions may be different also. For example, shock and denial will most likely last longer with a sudden death. Unfortunately, the cycles through the various emotions tend to occur at rapid-fire rates when the time available is short. Clients who have been in these situations have described such a short grieving time as riding a roller coaster of emotions.

John and Cindy were called to the hospital at 11 PM on a Saturday night. Their nineteen-year-old son, Josh, had been the victim of a hit-and-run accident and was unconscious. The prognosis was grim: He had suffered massive brain injury such that, even if he lived, he would be completely paralyzed and unable to speak or eat. While cycling through the anticipatory grieving stages at lightning speed, John and Cindy had to make momentous decisions. Should the ventilator be continued? If his condition stabilized and the ventilator could be removed, should a feeding tube be surgically inserted? How could they care for him, perhaps for years? Should they remove all life support and let nature take its course? There never are any simple answers to these questions. Many of these decisions would have been easier if Josh had made his wishes known to his family, but at nineteen, Josh had not even considered planning for his death. While making these extremely difficult decisions, John and Cindy experienced the emotions of anticipatory grieving: There would be no college education, no graduation ceremony, no marriage, no grandchildren. Clearly, the decisions families make at this time have an impact on grief emotions.

A family's individual circumstances and beliefs play crucial roles in these decisions. John and Cindy called on support from their extended family, friends, and their priest. In their situation, they did not want opinions from their supporters about what to do; they simply wanted the comfort of knowing that their friends were present.

What You Should Know during the Anticipatory Grieving Stage

As someone who supports a friend who is dying, or who supports the dying person's family, you need to understand the stages of grief outlined in chapter 1. You need to be able to recognize behaviors and words that tell you how someone is feeling, even when the person may not recognize the emotions. A clue that folks are experiencing the anger stage of grief includes the person lashing out at inappropriate people—the medical profession, the dying person, or God. For most of our clients, anticipatory grief anger is a difficult stage. Consequently, it is a difficult stage for supporters of those who are grieving. We are not supposed to be angry with someone who is dying or angry with God. Be available to let your friend rant and rave toward you, and simply accept the anger. If the person remembers the outburst later, you can accept an apology. If she does not, forget the incident ever happened.

When a person says he wishes there were things he had said to or done for his loved one—or not said or done—he is probably feeling some guilt. Ideally, this is the time when the dying person, and those who love him, can take care of unfinished business. As a friend, you can encourage your friend to do so. Sometimes a person experiencing anticipatory grief will become ill with a cold or a stress-related illness. He may awaken at night with nightmares, having a panic attack. It is often difficult to watch someone cry who is depressed or sad. We want them to stop, to feel better. Let the person cry. Tears are often the best catharsis for emotion.

You do not need to do anything to try to change the person's feelings. You merely need to accept them. Just being present provides comfort. But know when not to be present. Ultimately, those who walk the path of grief do so alone. As much as we want to help and comfort, there are times when we cannot. It is almost never wrong to ask if your presence is wanted or needed. Honor the person's wishes, even when you think the person does not himself know what he needs. You can always ask again later.

Know your friend's customs about dying and death. Sometimes those beliefs are radically different from yours. Accept and honor them. Beliefs are not right or wrong. They are just different. For example, Deb comes from a large extended family that gathers when death is imminent. This gathering of the clan is comforting and supportive for her. Her friend Frances, however, believes that death should be treated quietly. When Frances's husband was dying, she requested that no one come to the hospital so that she could be alone with him. Again, ask.

Know your friend's spiritual beliefs about dying, death, and afterlife. You do not need to agree with his beliefs, but you do need to be sensitive to them and honor them. Now is not the time to try to convert someone to your belief system. Norma, a Pentecostal Christian, visited a coworker whose wife was dying. Norma knew the family was Jewish, which she chose to ignore. "I'm sure Jesus is waiting for her in heaven," Norma said to her coworker. He, of course, was appalled and angered at her lack of sensitivity to his family's beliefs.

Examine your relationship to the grieving person and her family. Is this someone with whom you have a close enough relationship that you can be emotionally available to her, or is this a coworker you are fond of, but whose home you have never visited?

Are you able to listen without judgment or comment? More important, are you able to listen without comparing your friend's situation to prior situations in your own life? Are you able to avoid saying, "I know just how you feel?" You can *never* know exactly how someone else feels.

What You Should Do during the Anticipatory Grieving Stage

This section contains suggestions that are by no means exhaustive; they act as a guide to spur you to think about the needs of both the caretakers and the dying person. Again, the best policy is to ask what is needed. There are times, however, when your friend does not really know what she needs because she is not thinking clearly. Making suggestions is acceptable. Other times, your friend may not be able to ask for help because she feels she should be strong. It is okay to suggest that she allow assistance.

If you are comfortable helping your friend or the person who is dying create a legacy of his life, your assistance might be valuable to the family. For years, the Smith family had been planning to tape a family discussion regarding the family tree, but had never gotten around to it. As their grandmother was approaching her final days of cognition, she asked the family to gather for this talk. Bert, a family friend, operated the video camera during the event so that the family members could be together.

It is also important to volunteer to do what you are truly willing and able to do. Do not volunteer to feed the dog if you dislike the dog. If sitting with a dying person is emotionally impossible for you, do not offer to do it. Most likely, you will be miserable, may do something wrong, and might become resentful. Most important, the people you wish to help will sense your true feelings.

Again, depending on your relationship with the person in need, you may do things without asking or being told. You see tasks that need to be accomplished, and you do them. Also, you should realize that as the illness progresses, the needs of the family will change. What may not be needed today may be needed tomorrow.

Depending on the individual situation, many of the tasks listed below need to be accomplished. As death draws closer, however, some of these tasks can fall by the wayside, while others become more important. In the last few days or hours of a person's life, priorities change radically. For example, the cat still needs to be fed, but sweeping the kitchen floor can wait.

Household chores
- Wash the dishes and clean the kitchen.
- Vacuum, sweep, mop, dust.
- Take out the trash (to the curb on pickup day).
- Take out or deliver recycled items.
- Clean the bathrooms.
- Change the linens and do the laundry.
- Feed the pets.
- Walk the dog.
- Clean the cat box.
- Water the plants.
- Mow the grass and weed the flower beds.
- Fill the wildlife feeders.
- Bring in the mail and newspapers.
- Sweep or shovel the snow from walkways.
- Arrange for prepared meals to be brought in.

Errands
- Transport the children to school, soccer games, dance lessons, etc.

❧ Shop for groceries, toiletries, paper products, and
   cleaning supplies.
❧ Drop off or pick up prescriptions and medical supplies.
❧ Go to the post office or bank.
❧ Take the pets to the veterinarian.
❧ Service and gas the car.
❧ Transport to doctor's appointments.

Stock the house

❧ Paper products (tissues, cups, plates, paper towels, toilet
   paper, etc.).
❧ Bottled water.
❧ Other drinks (juices, teas, coffees, coffee filters, etc.).
❧ Simple meals that can be frozen and thawed quickly.
❧ Healthy snack foods (junk food may be okay too).
❧ Notepads, pens, pencils next to the telephones.

Other helpful suggestions (if desired by your friend)

❧ Check telephone messages.
❧ Check e-mail messages.
❧ Make telephone calls.
❧ Give your friend a blank book for journaling.
❧ Send cards that simply say "I'm thinking about you"
❧ Sit with the dying person. (Caution: be sure you are
   fully informed as to what is needed for this task. For
   example, do not lift the patient if you are not trained to
   do so. Know how you feel about sitting with a dying
   person. If you are uncomfortable, this task is best left to
   someone else.) You may read to the person, give him a
   hand massage with lotion, or play cards or a board game
   with him, if he chooses.
❧ Say good-bye to the dying person. Say how much the
   dying person means to you. Hospice literature abounds
   with documentation that dying persons can hear even if
   they appear unconscious. The closure is important not
   only to the dying person, but also to you.

If the dying person is away from home (in the hospital,
a hospice care center, a nursing home, etc.):

  ❧ Provide food and drinks for the family at the facility, if
     allowed
  ❧ Bring a toiletry kit for family members who are sitting
     with the patient
  ❧ Provide notepaper and pens to log calls and visitors
  ❧ Run errands
  ❧ Transport children or elderly friends to the facility

Do for yourself

  ❧ Set boundaries about what you are willing to do.
  ❧ Set limits for yourself as to how much time you are
     willing to give.
  ❧ Set a schedule for yourself as to when you are available
     to help; then be there when you say you will.
  ❧ If you find yourself in a position of organizing others,
     delegate.
  ❧ Know when to leave and then do so.

What You Should Not Do
during the Anticipatory Grieving Stage

When Ted's mother was unconscious and dying in a hospital, two
of her acquaintances from church came to visit. Ted, an only child
whose father had died several years before, had only met these
ladies once previously. They came into the hospital room, introduced themselves, and sat down in the only chairs in the room. They
did not speak to his mother. For several minutes, Ted made small
talk with them, then began hinting that he wished to be alone with
his mother. Other relatives began to arrive, and still these women
made no move to leave, or even to relinquish their seats to Ted's
elderly aunt. Finally, after more than an hour, Ted thanked them for
coming and asked them to leave. They did, highly insulted. Do not
overstay your welcome. Do not make family members feel like they

need to entertain you. Do not feel like you need to be present for a "deathbed" scene. Outlined below are additional suggestions about what not to do during the anticipatory grieving stage.

Unless you are asked to do so, avoid doing the following:
- ❧ Telling your own grieving stories
- ❧ Saying you know how someone feels—you can never know
- ❧ Dropping in without calling, unless you are extremely close friends.
- ❧ Opening the mail
- ❧ Turning on the television, radio, stereo, or computer
- ❧ Sitting for long periods of time (unless you are asked to do so), and bringing something with you to do (a book, needlework, etc.)
- ❧ Getting in the middle of family discussions or controversy
- ❧ Getting in the middle of family discussions with healthcare professionals
- ❧ Expressing your opinion about anything regarding patient care, the emotional state of family members, or relationships among family members. You will end up being the one who is alienated.

One final suggestion—be a friend. You have been this person's friend under better circumstances. You know and love this person who is in so much pain. Put your own needs on a back burner for a while. The ultimate behavior of friendship is to be there and allow your friend to feel, think, and do whatever he needs to get through this difficult time. Remember, simply being there is better than saying or doing anything else.

Chapter 3

Between Death
and the Ceremony

Traditions, practices, and beliefs vary greatly concerning that time between the moment of death and the disposition of the body. Again, there are no rights and wrongs. Folks generally handle this time the way their family, religious beliefs, and culture have always handled them. Conversely, some people may ignore their customs or their practices, deviating from the norm because their personal beliefs are different from the society in which they live. The circumstances surrounding death—the age of the person, the relationship between the deceased person and others, and the length of preparation time—determine how this period is treated. Also, individual shock, denial, and erupted emotions play critical roles in how one addresses this time immediately after death.

Emotional and Household Needs between Death and the Ceremony

Those first few minutes and hours after death have for many people a surrealistic feeling. Some of us do not remember this time later; it is a kaleidoscope of muffled sounds and images. Others can, even years later, describe this time in vivid detail, explaining exactly what was said, who was there, and even what clothes they were wearing. These responses are a result of the initial shock and denial stage that comes immediately after a death.

For Kay and Mike, those first few hours after their father's death were crystal clear. They had sat vigil at their father's hospital bed for four days while he was unconscious in the final stages of bone cancer. Mike would not leave the room for a minute, Kay for only brief periods of time. Finally, a skillful hospice social worker was able to help them understand that their father might want them to leave, that he would not die with them present in the room. They finally agreed to leave early in the evening, but only if someone they trusted and their father loved would sit vigil for them. They asked their cousin if she would be willing to stay with him during those last hours. She willingly did so, and their father died peacefully at 2:30 AM. Their cousin, as agreed, called Mike, who in turn called Kay. Kay knew immediately what the ringing telephone meant. When she lifted the receiver, Mike said simply, "It's over." He couldn't bring himself to say the word *dead*.

The brother and sister met at the hospital. Kay said that in her shock she did not realize that her dad's body would still be lying in the bed; she thought he would already be taken to the morgue. Instead, the hospital staff had bathed and straightened him, his hands folded and his face finally at peace.

With hardly a glance at his father, Mike began to pack his father's belongings, needing desperately to keep busy. Kay on the other hand kissed her father on the forehead, and told him how peaceful he looked. They signed the necessary papers and left before the mortuary staff arrived. Kay said later, "The body in that bed was not my dad. I felt no need to stay."

Years later, Kay could remember every detail of the three days between Mike's phone call and the evening after the funeral. "I needed to hold that time close because, in some way, it allowed me to continue to hold my dad close."

Betty has no memory of those first few hours after her husband's death. Tom collapsed on the bathroom floor at home, suffering a heart attack. Betty called 911, and Tom was rushed to the hospital. She and their fourteen-year-old son, Kevin, followed in their car. Betty refused to leave the emergency department cubicle while the team worked on Tom. She heard the doctor pronounce him dead, but the words did not register. She held his hand, unaware of its increasing coldness, and repeatedly said to hospital staff, "He's resting. He's going to wake up soon, and we'll go home." After two hours, a hospital chaplain was called in, but she was unable to help Betty understand that Tom was really dead, and that his body needed to be moved. She asked about family members or friends who might come to the hospital to help, but Kevin explained that they had moved to the area only a few weeks earlier, and their closest relatives were several states away. Finally, after six hours at the bedside, Kevin was able to make his mom leave. Betty obviously was in deep shock and denial, exacerbated by isolation in a strange city with no support. The loving hospital chaplain arranged for a minister of Betty's denomination and his congregation to support the family after they left the hospital.

Jennifer, ten years old, had battled leukemia for some time. As the end drew near, she was placed in a hospice care center where her parents, brother and sister, and many other relatives and friends could be with her and comfort each other. Jennifer died early on a Friday evening. By the time her parents made necessary arrangements at the care center and returned home, the house was full of friends, coffee was brewed, and sandwiches were ready.

Jennifer and her family belonged to a strong southern Protestant tradition in which extended family and friends pitched in to do whatever was necessary during the three days between death and the funeral. Friends shared the responsibility of greeting guests, tidying the kitchen, recording food contributions and phone calls, cleaning the bathrooms, and emptying the trash. Jennifer's immediate family was never left alone because their friends wanted to anticipate the family's every need; their friends responded in the tradition of their beliefs.

In the old South, customs are deeply ingrained and resentments can be held for years if protocol is not followed. Roberta remembers those days between her fiancé's death and his memorial service as a time of gentle caring and soft tears, except for one incident. Her supervisor at work, a woman from a different tradition and area of the country, came to Roberta's home to pay her respects. She thrust a boxed grocery store cake at Roberta, saying, "Everybody at work said I was supposed to bring something to eat. I don't understand why, but here's a cake." Roberta decided at that moment she could no longer work with someone so disrespectful, and she quit her job soon thereafter. Incidentally, no one ate the cake.

Individual and cultural beliefs must be respected, even when those beliefs appear superstitious or foreign to our own traditions. For example, many Irish families turn mirrors toward the wall to avoid seeing evil spirits. Some cultures do not allow the grieving family to mention the deceased person's name for a period of time.

People exhibit many different emotions during this time. As mentioned, shock and denial are usually present, especially if the death came suddenly. Crying, screaming, and flailing about are not uncommon. Such a display of emotion can be a means of sharing the burden and of lessening the intensity of the feelings. There is a sense of unreality, or denial, that the person is really gone. Conrad had spoken to his brother by phone every night at six o'clock throughout his long stay in a nursing home. For the first few evenings after his brother's death, Conrad's urge to dial his brother's number was overwhelming. "I had to dial the number and hear the recording 'this number is no longer in service' before I could admit he was dead."

Sometimes the relief that the person has died is overwhelming, particularly when the deceased has suffered tremendously. It is acceptable for family members to express that relief. Ironically, humor is also often present. This can be a time of telling wonderful, humorous stories about the deceased person. This reminiscent laughter is not disrespectful—it can be healing.

Other traditions, however, hold that those first few days after a death should be quiet, introspective times, perhaps with only the immediate family present. Visits to the survivor's home may not be welcome. A grieving person may waver between telling friends to "go home and leave me alone" and "please stay by my side." One of our clients said she needed friends and family in the house during those days, but also needed time to be alone. She took lots of showers, where she could be alone with her grief while others remained in the house. You should respect your friend's wishes and customs, although it is not inappropriate to ask if you can help in some way. It is almost always thoughtful to send a card.

Another consideration during this time concerns family members and friends who come from out of town for the service. There may be accommodation and transportation needs. Again, it is acceptable to ask how you can help.

Childcare issues may arise. If you are willing to assist with this task, read the chapter on children and grief before you volunteer.

Families frequently have financial problems during this time, particularly when the death is unexpected. It depends on your relationship with your friend and his family how you approach giving or helping to find financial support for him. A minister, priest, or rabbi might be helpful in quietly arranging donations for the family. Many local charities have funds for assisting in emergencies as well.

Planning the Disposition
Even if prior arrangements have been made, there are still some items that the family must attend to after the death of a loved one.

Typically, the family member who has legal authority to make decisions, along with whoever else chooses to participate, meets with a representative of the mortuary. This meeting, usually held at the mortuary, can be emotionally draining because the family members involved are still in shock and denial. Decisions have to be made that are difficult at best. Depending on the situation, this meeting may take about an hour.

Planning for disposition of a loved one's body can be extremely stressful on family members. Friends need to be aware of this and provide gentle support to the grieving family members. Usually, someone needs to be present in the home to receive calls and friends who may drop by while your friend is meeting with the mortuary staff.

Unfortunately, this planning process can also be cause for tremendous tension among family members. Various family members have their individual ideas about how or if a service is to be carried out, what kind of casket to buy, and a myriad of other decisions. Money is often a factor in this conflict. Mortuaries charge for each service rendered, some of which are expensive. Bizarre as this next story sounds, it is true.

Dora's husband had told her he wanted to be cremated and his ashes scattered on the family farm. Unfortunately, he did not tell his adult children his desire. While Dora agreed to his wishes, she privately thought cremation would not exhibit to her friends and family how much she loved her husband. She believed in the notion that the more one spends on a funeral, the more love for the deceased is shown. She did indeed arrange for cremation but kept this secret from her family. She paid for embalming (not required for cremation in the state in which she lived) and purchased an expensive marble casket. The family had a "family night" viewing of the body at the mortuary. After the viewing, the body was removed from the casket and cremated. A closed-casket graveside service was held at the town cemetery the next day. The empty marble casket was buried, with many comments from extended family and friends about how Dora had spared no expense for her husband's funeral. Several days later she gathered her children and told them the truth, explaining that they now needed to conduct a private ceremony to scatter their father's ashes. Her children were appalled. Not only had they endured a fake funeral, but they now had to go through another closure event. Worse, Dora had spent thousands of dollars on funeral costs that their father had not wanted her to spend.

Obviously, tremendous conflict arose among Dora's children, and between some of them and Dora. After the initial shock, two of the children understood and supported her decision, three others were angry and felt deceived. Many years later, the family factions were still at war.

Your job as a supporter of someone who grieves is to stay out of family conflicts. Ultimately, the family's problems are not yours. Try hard not to take sides.

Flowers, Gifts, Memorials, and Cards

More and more families are requesting that flowers not be sent when a loved one dies. In his PBS television series, Bill Moyers discussed this trend, lamenting this lack of tangible evidence of condolence. He cited the millions of flowers given to the British royal family when Princess Diana died as society's need to express sympathy. He said he found it ironic that we could send flowers to the grieving British royal family, which actually is unknown intimately to us, but we could not do so for people we love.

One trend today is to send a memorial monetary contribution to a charity suggested by the family. If your friend requests this, do so. The custom is to send an amount equal to about what you would have paid for flowers. Typically, the organization receiving your gift will send a note to the family letting them know you made a contribution (amount is usually not stated), and it will send you an acknowledgement of receipt.

Do not send a contribution to the charity of *your* choice, unless the family specifically states that doing so is acceptable to them.

You actually may offend your friend if you do. For example, Irma sends a contribution to a local Christian orphanage when someone dies, regardless of the wishes of the family. When a Moslem friend lost a relative recently, he asked that memorials be made to the local hospice organization. Irma sent her usual contribution to the orphanage. When her friend received the note from the orphanage, he was incensed that Irma has been so insensitive, blatantly ignoring both his request and his religious and cultural heritage.

Financial gifts are sometimes acceptable and appreciated. As mentioned earlier, death is expensive. Depending on the family's circumstances and your relationship with the family, a monetary contribution may be perfectly appropriate. You may give money directly to your friend, or if you are uncomfortable doing so, give it to the minister, priest, or rabbi to pass on to the family.

Another way to contribute financially is by providing household items. As noted in chapter 2, many of these items may need to be stocked if large numbers of people are expected at the home during this time. When Joan's brother died, more than two hundred people filled her home during the three days between his death and funeral. That's a lot of toilet paper.

Food is one of the most culturally bound components of the early stages of grieving. In Deb's southern tradition, people bring food and everyone eats, and then eats some more. As her friend Terri says, "What's a funeral without fried chicken?" The ostensible reason for bringing food to the family is so they will not have to think about meal preparation during this period, but the tradition goes deeper than that. Funerals are often a time when extended family members and friends gather, even when they do not usually see each other under other circumstances. Food is a symbol of hospitality. Food is comfort. Food is a type of reminiscing: "Mama loved Aunt Mabel's deviled eggs! She always made them for the Easter picnic."

The family sometimes has unusual eating habits during this time, so try not to be offended if the family does not dive right into your dish. When Ed's wife died, he found he could not eat meat for about three months after her death. Bring food that either does not have to be refrigerated or can be frozen and eaten later. The September 2000 edition of *Southern Living* has an article on suggested dishes to take to a friend's house after a death. Either bring your offering in a container that does not have to be returned or clearly mark your name on the dish and come back for it a few days later. Remember that having to return containers adds an additional burden on the family.

Some families, however, do not hold with the food traditions noted above. For many families, having people in their home and food brought in feels like a burden. You should call ahead to see if the family is receiving food. A growing trend is for the family and close friends to host a reception after the service. We recently attended such a reception in the church fellowship hall after the memorial service, complete with a champagne toast for the deceased. In some Jewish congregations, and in some areas of the country, food is not brought to the family until after the service. In a later chapter, we will discuss the need for food gifts long after the ceremony is over.

What if There Is No Ceremony or if It Is Held Far Away?

A memorial service or funeral brings some sense of closure for the family and friends of the deceased in most cultures. It also is a way of celebrating the person's life. However, there is a growing trend for either a private family ceremony or none at all.

Again, the best course of action is to ask what the family desires. Sometimes, even when the ceremony is to be private, at a later time, or in a distant location, the family still wishes to have friends gathered around them for a few days. They also may want memorial gifts sent to a charity. Other times, the family wishes no one outside the immediate family to be present.

If your friend must travel to a distant location for the event, offer to housesit for him and follow most of the suggestions listed in chapter 2 for ways you can help while your friend is out of town.

Allen's grandmother died at age 102. Her instructions were explicit to him: "I've outlived anybody who cares whether or not I'm dead, except you. I lived. I died. I don't believe in the here-after. I'll just be dead. Cremate me and bury my ashes somewhere. No urn. No memorial service. No headstone. Just a death certificate and a one-paragraph obituary for legal purposes." Allen followed her wishes. However, he did need support for himself during this time, and his friends rallied.

Depending on the individual circumstances, most of the "to-do" and "not-to-do" suggestions listed in chapter 2 can be followed during this time between death and the ceremony. Outlined below are some additional suggestions that are particular to this time. Again, keep in mind that your relationship with your friend determines which of these tasks are appropriate for you.

What You Should Do
between Death and the Ceremony
Household chores

- ❧ Keep a record of phone calls.
- ❧ Greet visitors (if there is a guest book, ask them to sign it).
- ❧ Keep a record of floral gifts, if received (mortuaries usually provide record books for this).
- ❧ Bring food and beverages, if desired.
- ❧ Keep a record of food, beverage, and household supply contributions, and make a note of any containers that need to be returned.
- ❧ Prepare and serve food and beverages.
- ❧ Handle food storage.
- ❧ Inventory needed household supplies.
- ❧ Housesit while the family is away from home.

Errands

- ❧ Transport out-of-town friends and relatives from airports to hotels, the home, and the service.
- ❧ Shop for or borrow needed household items. (For example, you may need to borrow a large coffee maker from a church or restaurant).
- ❧ Transport or baby-sit children (see the chapter on children and grief).

Other "to-do's"

- ❧ Tell your friend, repeatedly, to call you if she needs you.
- ❧ Follow the family's wishes regarding flowers and memorial gifts.
- ❧ Give monetary support, if appropriate.
- ❧ Contribute to the suggested charity.
- ❧ Send a condolence card, even if you have been present.
- ❧ Give your friend a blank book for journaling during the grieving process.
- ❧ Call potential pallbearers, if the family requests you to do so.
- ❧ Call the deceased person's friends to notify them of time of service(s).
- ❧ Set up appointments for meeting with the mortuary.

What not to do between death and the ceremony

- ❧ Do not come to the home if the family desires privacy.
- ❧ Do not get in the middle of family discussions or planning.
- ❧ Do not get involved in family conflicts.
- ❧ Do not bring food or other items if the family asks that none be brought.
- ❧ Do not bring food that needs to be refrigerated and cannot be frozen for later use.
- ❧ Do not contribute to the charity of your choice, unless you are sure this is acceptable to the family.

❧ Do not bring your children to the home unless you are certain the family welcomes them (Children running through the house are often not wanted.)

❧ Do not overstay your welcome (Attention spans tend to be brief for people who are in shock. Also, if there are many other people present, your friend needs to spend a little time with everyone.)

❧ Bite your tongue if you're about to offer a cliché such as "she's in a better place" or "it was God's will."

The time between death and disposition of the body is filled with many emotions for family and loved ones. Remember that grief can cloud your friend's judgment so that she makes emotional decisions that may not be logical. While your friend may not know she needs assistance, it is important to have a trustworthy person help with decisions. Your sensitivity and compassion will almost certainly be remembered long after the ceremony takes place. Step outside yourself for a while and concentrate on your friend's needs. If you do not know for certain, ask.

Chapter 4

The Ceremony and Immediately After

A closure ritual, either immediately before death or soon after someone dies, is found in almost every culture and belief system. For some, this rite celebrates or commemorates the deceased person's life; for others, it helps guide the deceased to an afterlife. This event varies greatly, depending on cultural norms and religious beliefs. The information presented in this chapter offers general information only and is meant to be a basic guideline to various customs—your friend's tradition may be dramatically different from the norm of his or her belief system. Your role as a friend, first and foremost, is to be present at the ceremony if your friend wishes you to be present, and to respect your friend's individual practices.

Religious Traditions

Traditions vary widely concerning closure ceremonies. In the Jewish tradition, for example, the body may not be embalmed (except where tradition is overruled by state law) and must be buried within twenty-four hours after death. A body cannot be buried on the Sabbath, however, so burial sometimes must take place on the same day as the death, particularly in the Orthodox tradition. Some reformed and conservative congregations may wait until the day after the Sabbath, depending upon the circumstances.

The traditional European American Christian procedure is to conduct a closure ceremony about three days after death. In some African American Christian denominations, burial may not be until about a week after death. This usually allows time for relatives and friends traveling to the service to arrive. In both communities, however, the rites themselves vary widely.

In most liturgical Christian denominations (such as Catholic, Episcopal, Lutheran, and Presbyterian), the ceremony is fairly somber, with the congregation participating in prayers, responsive readings, and singing. The eulogy is usually short. Sometimes friends and family members present a reading or say a few words. In nonliturgical Protestant denominations (Southern Baptist and United Methodist), the ceremony varies greatly, depending upon the particular church. Sometimes soloists perform, and the eulogy tends to be a bit longer.

In almost all Christian churches, the style of memorializing the deceased is changing. For example, one part of the ceremony historically took place in the church, with the casket present. Often the casket was opened at the church for a final viewing of the deceased. Then the casket was closed and transported to the gravesite, and a second, shorter ceremony was conducted before burial. Now, the ceremony often takes place only in a mortuary or only at the gravesite. Because the number of people choosing cremation has increased dramatically, fewer families go to the expense of two services. Also, because of cremation, many folks choose nontraditional locations for services, such as the deceased person's favorite park, the beach, or the mountains. Today, services may be conducted by someone other than a member of the clergy.

The issue of burial versus cremation has its roots in the basic tenets of each denomination's beliefs. Advent Christians, for example, believe that the dead are asleep until Jesus's second coming and discourage cremation. Eastern Orthodox, Greek Orthodox, Russian Orthodox, Church of Jesus Christ of Latter Day Saints, Church of God, and others also frown upon cremation. Conversely, Unitarian Universalists, Christian Scientists, and others allow and sometimes encourage cremation.

Lynn and her husband were members of a Christian denomination that preferred burial; however, their individual preference was cremation. When Lynn's husband died, she followed his wishes. She arrived at the church with her husband's urn in her arms and asked the minister where she should place it for the ceremony. Lynn's husband was the first congregant to be cremated. The minister was so distraught about her "breaking the rules" that he screamed at her, "I don't care where you put him. Just drop him somewhere!" Lynn lovingly placed the urn on the altar, seething inside at the minister's insensitivity. She said in retrospect, "The minister knew what to do with a big coffin but had no idea how to handle a small box. I know I went against my denomination's beliefs, but I had to follow my husband's desire."

In African American denominations, customs also vary greatly. Some traditions, however, are rooted in a need to dignify the dead, who may not have been treated with respect while alive. According to psychologist Ronald Barrett[1] in a speech presented in 1994 at the Association of Death Education and Counseling national conference, African Americans spend more money on memorializing the dead than do any other minority. He stated that such a large expenditure is symbolic of honoring the deceased. African Americans are less likely than European Americans to choose cremation, preferring to have the body visible for a wake and the funeral. Expression of emotion and singing are often a part of the African American funeral experience.

Within the Christian community, several denominations do not observe closure rituals or last rites before death. The Armenians and several Orthodox sects consider Holy Communion to be the last rite. Christian Scientists, Church of Christ, Church of God, Grace Brethren, Jehovah's Witnesses, Nazarenes, and others do not traditionally observe last rites.

Customs vary widely in other religions. In the Baha'i faith, for example, prayer and fasting occur as the person is dying. There are no last rites. Buddhists chant at the bedside as the person is dying, and then the body is cremated. In the Black Muslim belief, there is a special procedure for washing and shrouding the dead. In the Islamic/Muslim belief, the family washes and prepares the body for death, and the body is placed facing Mecca. In the Hindu tradition, a priest ties a thread around the dying person's wrist or neck, signifying a blessing. When the person dies, the priest pours water into his mouth.[2]

Some people follow their religious beliefs and customs exactly, carrying out age-old rituals for a variety of reasons. Others observe death rituals in ways that are most comfortable to them regardless of religious doctrines. Keith's mother was a member of a church that permitted only sacred music at funerals. His mother, however, had requested that he arrange to have an Elvis Presley song sung at her service. He knew she would have liked one of Elvis's love songs, but he requested a soloist to sing "Precious Lord, Take My Hand," which Elvis recorded on his Christmas album. He had managed to stay within the doctrine of his mother's church, while simultaneously honoring her request.

Regardless of your friend or coworker's beliefs, or the rituals performed, you have an obligation to respect and honor them, whether or not you agree with them. You also have a responsibility to keep any negative thoughts and opinions about the ceremony to yourself.

Secular Ceremonies

A growing number of people in America today are unchurched (i.e., having no religious affiliation). Closure ceremonies among this population vary widely, depending on individual preference. Deb recently attended such a memorial service for a woman she knew quite well. The event took place on the beach at sunset. Friends and family members recited poems, spoke eulogies for the deceased, sang her favorite songs, and lighted candles for her. Her husband waded into the breakers and scattered her ashes into the falling tide.

A growing number of families choose to have private closure ceremonies with no one outside the family in attendance. Certainly, you should honor the family's wishes; however, at an appropriate time, do send a card or call on the family to express your condolences.

Whatever the family's choice regarding a closure ceremony, your responsibility is to attend and to follow the rituals set forth.

Emotional Impacts of the Ceremony

For some people, the anticipation of the ceremony is more painful than the ceremony itself—the service brings relief from the period of shock. For others, the ceremony hurts horribly—closure is unwanted and too final. While Meg was being ushered into the church for her fiancé's memorial service, she screamed at the mortuary employee guiding her, "Mister, I'm not going in there! You can't make me!"

Pat said he remembered only the exquisite details of the petals of a yellow rose in the altar arrangement at his son's funeral. He had no memory of anything the priest said or of the songs that were sung. Conversely, Diane remembered vividly the minister's eulogy for her sister. "He really knew her, really loved her, and his words genuinely reflected his caring."

Ron, his family, and their minister wanted his mother's service to be a celebration of his mom's life. The minister's eulogy reflected their desire. He told stories of meals shared, jokes told, and tears cried around her kitchen table. After the ceremony, one of Ron's coworkers told him he wished he had known his mother.

"That was the highest compliment anyone could give my mom, my family, and our minister."

Emotional displays at closure ceremonies vary, depending on the individual and upon the beliefs of the religious organization. For example, animated gesturing is often exhibited in some Pentecostal and African American churches. In some churches, designated church members stand by the family members' pews, waving fans should the bereaved be overcome with emotion. In other denominations, quiet stoicism is the norm. Again, there are no rights or wrongs in expressing emotion. People do what they need to do.

Your Responsibility during the Ceremony

Go to the service—the family will appreciate your presence. If there is a guest book at the door, sign it. The family may not remember you being present, and reading signatures later is a comfort to them. Often, the family takes a head count during a closure ceremony. Sometimes unspoken, this counting numbers in attendance is a means of measuring love, respect, caring, and popularity of both the deceased and his family. Joan, who was mentioned in chapter 3, lost her brother, and about two hundred people came to his funeral. Joan asked her office-mate George after the death of his mother, "How many people attended her funeral?" He replied proudly, "At least forty." Joan thought to herself, "Poor woman, she didn't have many friends." In actuality, George's mother was ninety years old, had recently moved from another city, and had lost many of her peers to death. Forty people in attendance at her funeral really was remarkable. In Joan's culture, the number of people attending the ceremony is a symbol of how well loved and respected the deceased was. While the number of people attending a funeral or memorial service really is not an affirmation of the deceased person's life, grieving relatives often view large numbers in attendance as such.

Follow the order of service. Even if you do not know (or believe in) the songs or prayers, stand or kneel silently with the congregation. Doing so is respectful. Sit in an appropriate section of the sanctuary. Usually, the front few pews are reserved for family members.

Wear appropriate attire. In most American cultures today, this no longer means black, but you should ask. Deb attended a funeral recently where a young woman was dressed in shorts and a tank top. There was more discussion after the ceremony about her clothes than about the deceased!

If you cannot, for whatever reason, attend the service, offer to housesit or sit with children, if they are not to attend. One of the many ills of American society today includes funeral theft. Houses left unattended during a ceremony are often the targets of theft. You could assist with meal preparation while the family is at the service.

Immediately after the Ceremony

Traditions are changing today about this period of time. Historically, those attending the service went to a family member's home for a meal after the service. In most Jewish sects, a meal is prepared for the family by members of the congregation. In others, the family provides the meal for guests. In the South, food is prepared by friends and church members for the family and guests. A recent trend away from this custom is a reception in the church fellowship hall or a gathering of family and close friends at a restaurant. At either, it would be complete with a receiving line.

Often a second guest register is present at the home or at the reception. Sign this one also. Certainly, feel free to eat, if food is present, but do not overindulge. Make sure there is enough to go around. Unless you are a close friend, do not stay too long. Remember that this has been a stressful day for your friend, and long conversations are emotionally draining.

What if There Is No Ceremony, or if the Ceremony Is in a Distant Location?

Reading the obituaries in your local newspaper can be enlightening about cultural trends in death practices. Frequently, obituaries state that "a private memorial service will be held at a later date" or "no services will be held." Whatever the family's choices, the body must be disposed of and emotions need to be addressed. Wait until a few days after you are sure the disposition has occurred, and send a card, or telephone. If you telephone, make the call brief (unless your friend wants to talk), saying simply that you are thinking of him. Your call or card may not necessarily be welcomed at the time, but you will have shown good manners.

What you should do during the ceremony
- ❧ Attend the service (if indoor and graveside services are held, attend both if possible).
- ❧ Offer to transport out-of-town guests or the elderly.
- ❧ Act as an usher or guestbook keeper if the family requests.
- ❧ Even if you are unwilling to participate in the rituals of the ceremony, be respectful: kneel, sit, and stand as others do.
- ❧ Sit in your proper place: remember the first few rows are reserved for family.
- ❧ Wear appropriate attire.
- ❧ If you cannot attend the service, offer to housesit or sit with children, if they are not attending.
- ❧ If you stay at the house, help prepare for guests.

What you should do immediately after the ceremony
- ❧ Transport guests to the reception location.
- ❧ Help with food preparation and serving.
- ❧ Greet guests and handle the guestbook, if requested by the family.
- ❧ Eat sparingly.

❧ Help with cleanup.

❧ Transport guests to lodging or the airport.

What you should not do during the ceremony

❧ Unless you are transporting guests, do not park too close to the building or gravesite—leave those spaces for the elderly or disabled.

❧ Do not expect to speak to the bereaved before or after the ceremony, unless a time has been set aside for this—they may be too distraught to cope with conversation.

❧ Do not bring small children to the ceremony, unless they were close to the deceased or your friend, and unless you have cleared it with the family prior to the ceremony.

❧ Do not make negative comments about the service.

What you should not do immediately after the ceremony

❧ Do not monopolize your friend's time—she has many people with whom she needs to speak.

❧ Do not overstay your welcome.

Ultimately, your responsibility as a friend to someone who is grieving is to be respectful and to honor the deceased. While the choices families make about disposition of the body and rituals may not be the same as yours, you are obligated to adhere to their wishes. What is important to your friend, both at the time and for a long time to come, is that you are present and that you care about his pain.

Chapter 5

The First Weeks
after Death

T he silence is overwhelming. The food is stored, the bathroom is clean, the rugs are vacuumed. The funeral wreath on the front door signifying death has been removed. Your friend is alone in the house for the first time, perhaps for the first time in a long while. The telephone does not ring because people are respecting her privacy. The chaos in which she has been living for the last few days is over. Now it is quiet.

Post-Death Grieving Stages

This is the time when emotions described by Westberg and Kübler-Ross begin to manifest themselves in full force. As with anticipatory grieving, the emotions spin in varying lengths of time. Some people cycle through several emotions in the course of an hour, others get stuck in a single emotion for long periods.

"I remember so clearly that first night alone after my husband died," Alma said. "We'd only spent a few nights apart in fifty-two years, when one of us was in the hospital. I thought I'd lose my mind in the silence. I wanted to scream, just to hear a voice."

This time of solitude is usually inevitable. It can be horribly painful. There are no words to describe the aching need to connect to someone, anyone. The shock and denial that have cushioned the loss through the memorial service have begun to subside. They are replaced by many emotions. Crying, screaming, and cursing sometimes erupt. "I believed I needed to be strong for my children during the days before and right after the funeral," Henry said after his wife died. "When I was finally alone, I could let myself sob in agony."

Anger may begin to surface. "About three days after my husband's funeral, the water heater broke. I sat on the floor in front of it, sobbing in impotent fury. I was so angry with him for not being there to fix it. I was angry at my inability to even know how to call someone to repair it. I was angry with God for taking him away. I felt furious to be so helpless. I was mad at the whole world," Alma said.

Depression and despair can appear fairly quickly after a death. Martha said, "After my daughter died I was plunged into darkness, both physically and emotionally. I felt as if I were living in a tunnel with no light at the end. I acted out those emotions by crying for hours in the dark. I couldn't switch on a light." Gwen manifested her depression after the death of her father by refusing to eat. "Everything I smelled made me sick. I couldn't stand the sight of meat. I lived for weeks on baked potatoes."

Others exhibit depression by withdrawing, not answering the door or telephone, or going out. Some drag themselves to work, using denial to get through the day. Then, upon arriving back home, they curl up in a ball and stare blankly at the walls, letting the depression take over again. The world seems overwhelming. "The first time I read a newspaper after my fiancé died, I was surprised to find life continued for others. War, famine, and politics still captured the news. The car crash in which he died was no longer news. It was as if my life—and his—were inconsequential," Vivian noted.

Illnesses frequently appear during the first week after loss. Dave said, "We buried my dad on a Monday. On Thursday, we took Mom to the hospital. She had double pneumonia." Gastrointestinal problems, headaches, nausea, and cardiovascular illnesses are usually symptoms of death-related stress.

Panic and anxiety are common. Vivian said she awoke every morning that first week at 3:14, the time of her fiancé's death. "I awoke gasping for breath, sweating all over. I had terrible nightmares, seeing him in grotesque dreams. The physical reality of his dead body was too much for me."

For some, the solitude of the first week after death brings an opportunity to reflect, which sometimes leads to guilt. "Did I do everything I could to save him? Did I tell him I loved him often enough, and could he hear me? Did I follow her wishes about the memorial service?"

"I felt crazy after my son died. I would beg God to kill me, and bring him back. I knew this attempt at bargaining with God was futile, but I couldn't stop myself," said Rob. Bargaining often is tied to guilt: "If only I had . . . he might have lived to graduate from high school."

Worden notes that the tasks of this early stage after death are to deal with the pain of the loss so that the pain can diminish over time. This is the time, according to Worden, that the bereaved person needs to deal with any unfinished business he may have had with the dead person. "I was sure my dad could still hear me after he died. I talked to him constantly, asking him to forgive me for any wrongs I did growing up. I know in my heart he forgave me," said Dave.

What Friends Can Do during the First Week after Death

For friends and coworkers, even if they have been intensely involved with the death and the death rituals, time moves on in the week after death. For the grieving person, time stands still. While the anticipation of death, the death itself, and the closure ritual were horribly difficult, the most arduous task is yet ahead. Grieving is hard work.

Send a handwritten note to your friend, even if you did so the day after the death. Telephone or visit your friend. Make the conversation brief. "I'm thinking about you," is all you need to say. Do not ask, "Is there anything I can do?" The answer will invariably be no, even when your friend needs much help. Do say, "Call me if you need anything." Your friend probably will not call. She probably does not have the emotional strength to pick up a telephone. Do say, "I'm going to the grocery store this afternoon. What can I pick up for you?" Avoid clichés. Don't say, "He's out of pain" or "It was for the best." How could you possibly know?

Accept your friend's silences. Often, words are too painful. On the contrary, if your friend wants to talk, listen. Do not change the subject. Accept tears. Let your friend cry. Accept anger. It is usually not really directed toward you. Simply listen. Allow your friend to change her mind about a subject in the middle of a sentence. Expect her to be forgetful. Memory loss after death is common. Do not probe for details about the death. That information is really none of your business. Never say, "I know how you feel" or "You must be feeling . . ." You do not know.

If you visit your friend with others present, do not talk to them about trivial matters, such as the weather, the stock market, or your favorite television program. Doing so negates your friend's feelings. "I thought I would scream at my friends' long discussion about the upcoming hurricane season after my granddad died," said Greg. "How could they focus on weather when I was hurting so badly?"

Do not pry. Now is not the time to ask, "What are you going to do with his clothes? Are you going to sell the house?" Worse, this is not the time to say, "Could I have his rods and reels?" In fact, if you must say something, encourage your friend to proceed slowly in making major decisions, if possible. Decisions made during this time are usually emotionally charged, and are not made with logic.

Do not make changes in your friend's home, such as hiding photographs or erasing the deceased person's voice from the answering machine. You have no right to do such things unless you are specifically asked. Your friend may engage in behaviors during this week that appear morbid to you, but are comforting to him. For example, Vivian sat for two hours each day at the location on the highway where her fiancé was killed. This need gradually diminished, but her friends thought it was weird while she needed to go to that place.

Unless you are a close friend who has been privy to personal information in the past, do not ask about financial issues. If you are in such a position, however, now might be the time your friend needs financial support. As noted in chapter 3, you can arrange for monetary assistance from friends, a religious organization, or social service agencies.

Even if your friend does not need money, she may need help in sorting through financial papers. If you are comfortable and competent in that area, you may offer to assist in this task. If you are not, suggest that she ask someone at her bank to help. This issue may surface particularly with elderly women, whose husbands traditionally managed all household finances. Alma confessed, "In fifty-two years, I'd never opened the phone bill, because it was addressed to my husband. He paid all the bills, handled all the insurance, and budgeted all our finances. The only checks I'd ever written were to the grocery store."

Do not place yourself in the middle of family discussions regarding financial or other matters. Keep your opinions to yourself unless you are asked and are sure that they will be well received. Ultimately, family decisions belong only to the family.

This is a time when your friend needs you to be a mind reader about household tasks, because he cannot think. Try to put yourself in your friend's shoes for a minute. For example, does the lawn need mowing? Does he have milk, eggs, and bread? Is the task of walking the dog overwhelming? Look back over the lists in previous chapters. Many of the tasks noted before death and near the memorial service continue to need to be accomplished.

"I will never need to buy another paper napkin, and I still have coffee in the freezer almost a year later," said Nora, "but I had no cat food, eggs, or bread the week after my husband's funeral. I simply had no strength to go grocery shopping. Fortunately, friends inventoried my kitchen, shopped for me, and put everything away."

"Although I'm very grateful for all the food and help before the funeral, if I never see another green bean casserole, it will be too soon," said Greg. "A friend brought over a giant chef's salad a few days after my grandfather died, and it is still the best thing I've ever eaten."

Suggestions for Employers and Coworkers during the First Week

Most American businesses provide three days of funeral leave or bereavement in their personnel policies. This practice, probably more than any other, speaks of our insensitivity and lack of respect for the pain grieving persons feel after a death. There is an unspoken (and sometimes spoken) notion that one should "be over it" in three days. Employers believe that an employee should be back to normal, productive, and responsible. How absurd! Most people are still in shock after three days, and have not even begun to feel the myriad of emotions that are going to flood them for a long time. Depending on the circumstances, two or three months may pass before the grieving person moves from shock to other grieving emotions. We urge employers to rethink this ridiculous policy.

Some companies allow employees to take sick leave or vacation leave for a brief period of time after the three days of bereavement are used, but often there are resentments and misunderstandings about how employees use this time. Also, many people unfortunately have used sick leave and vacation leave before the death and during the deceased person's illness, and there simply is no leave time available. While the federal Family Medical Leave Act has helped tremendously in this situation, not all employers are subject to its regulations. Additionally, even if an employer allows the employee time off without pay, the financial burden of taking this time off may be so great as to be prohibitive.

Some businesses have "shared leave" policies, in which employees may donate their accrued leave time to a coworker who needs additional time off. If your company has such a policy, donate some of your time. If your company does not have this policy, urge your employer to develop such a plan.

As an employer or supervisor, expect the reality that your employee is not back to her normal self. She may be unable to concentrate, forgetful, tearful, or short-tempered. Emotional outbursts, tardiness, and lethargy are normal. Overlook these behaviors—they will decrease in time. In later chapters, there are recommendations for employers if these behaviors do not diminish.

As a coworker, you might offer to take over some of the grieving person's responsibilities. You should set some boundaries on this, however. For example, you might say, "Let me handle the mail for you this first week" or "Let me handle this personnel issue for you."

Depending on your employing organization, your grieving coworker may need to talk about his experiences during breaks, at lunch, or after work. Be willing to listen. You do not have to respond or pass judgments. Simply listen. On the contrary, your coworker may not want to talk about his grief. If this is the case, don't pry. You might say, "If you need or want to talk, I'm willing to listen." If the reply is "No thanks, I'm okay," accept it. The need to talk may come later. Do not tell your coworker your own grieving stories. Right now, your friend does not care about deaths in your past, but only about the death in his family.

It is almost never wrong to say, "I'm sorry for your loss." Realize, however, that any kind words may send the grieving person into tears. Tears are okay. Allow the person to cry.

Rituals for the First Week after Death

Jewish sects probably have one of the best rituals we have heard of for the week after death. The ritual is called "sitting Shiva." Traditionally, the event was attended by family members and at least ten men, called a "minion." (This is still true in the Orthodox sect. In reformed and conservative congregations, women may now sit Shiva.) The rite is usually observed for seven days, excluding the Sabbath, although today the length of observance may be shorter in some congregations. Historically, those family members and friends sitting Shiva sat on hard seats (cardboard boxes are now provided by mortuaries). The doors to the home are left unlocked so that others can come and go, bringing food and greetings without disturbing those who are sitting. There are morning and evening services and prayers, with the rabbi sometimes in attendance.

The act of sitting Shiva allows the family members time for expressing grief and for reflecting about their loved one and their relationships to him. At the same time, they are not alone and their household needs are met. On the first Sabbath that the family attends a service after the death, the family is honored in the synagogue or temple and special prayers are given for the deceased and the family.

Most other religious groups do not have formal rituals for that first week after death; however, some people create rituals during this time. For example, during the first week after her mother's death, Deb kept a candle burning in her honor. She borrowed the tradition from the *yahrzeit* candle tradition in Judaism, in which a candle is lighted on the anniversary of the person's death and on special holidays.

Others need some kind of personal memorial event during this first week. Frank's granddaughter died during the summer. "We'd spent every summer of her short life walking on the beach, swimming, and collecting shells. Every day during those first few weeks after she died, I walked the beach, swam, and collected shells. There was something miraculously healing about diving into salt water, and I still have all the shells I collected in her memory."

Depending on the individual, and your relationship to her, you can gently offer suggestions about healthy rituals that she may want to develop during this first week. A symbol of her remembrance of the deceased may be comforting to her. Alma was a member of a garden club. After her husband died, the club planted a tree in a local park in his honor, had a ceremony dedicating the tree, engraved a marker with his name on it, and placed it beside the tree.

Deb's father loved Japan. During the week after his death, she developed plans for a Japanese garden dedicated to his memory. She spent the next year creating and planting it. Sue's mother was an avid birdwatcher. After her diagnosis of Alzheimer's disease and subsequent death, Sue took up bird watching in memory of her mother's interest.

Often, death occurs near or on special occasions such as birthdays, Christmas, or anniversaries. See the chapter on considerations for these events for suggestions about rituals for special occasions.

What you should do during the first week after death

- 〜 Send your friend a handwritten note stating that you are thinking about him and are sorry for his loss.
- 〜 Telephone your friend to say you are thinking of her.
- 〜 Make a brief visit to your friend's home.
- 〜 Listen to your friend if he needs to talk or cry.
- 〜 Be silent if your friend needs silence.
- 〜 Bring a food dish that you know is different from ones brought previously.
- 〜 Arrange for monetary support, if needed.

Household chores (if your friend desires your help)

- 〜 Wash the dishes and clean the kitchen.

❧ Vacuum, sweep, mop, dust.

❧ Take out the trash (to the curb on pickup day).

❧ Clean the bathrooms.

❧ Change the linens and do the laundry.

❧ Feed the pets.

❧ Walk the dog.

❧ Clean the cat box.

❧ Water the plants.

❧ Mow the grass and weed flower beds.

❧ Fill the wildlife feeders.

❧ Bring in the mail and newspapers.

❧ Sweep or shovel the snow from walkways.

❧ Arrange for prepared meals to be brought in.

Errands

❧ Transport the children to school, soccer games, dance lessons, etc.

❧ Shop for groceries, toiletries, and cleaning supplies

❧ Drop off or pick up prescriptions and medical supplies

❧ Go to the post office or bank

❧ Take the pets to the veterinarian

❧ Service and gas the car

❧ Transport your friend to doctor's appointments

What you should not do during the first week after death

❧ Do not ask personal questions, unless you are sure you have a relationship that warrants such questions.

❧ Do not make changes in the grieving person's home, unless you are asked to do so.

❧ Do not become involved in family discussions and decisions.

❧ Do not overstay your welcome.

❧ Do not change the topic of conversation if your friend needs to talk.

❧ Do not bring small children to the home unless you are sure they are welcome and unless you have cleared their presence with the family before you visit.

What employers and coworkers should do during the first week after death

- ❧ Employers should rethink bereavement policies (three days are often not enough for those suffering loss in the immediate family).
- ❧ Expect employees to be tearful, angry, forgetful, lethargic, tardy, or physically ill.
- ❧ Offer to share the grieving person's work load.
- ❧ Listen if the person needs to talk or cry.
- ❧ Mention the person who died by name (this acknowledges his existence and shows you care).

What employers and coworkers should not do during the first week after death

- ❧ Do not expect the person to be back to normal and fully functioning.
- ❧ Do not prevent the person from crying.
- ❧ Do not change the topic of conversation if the person needs to talk about the deceased.
- ❧ Do not avoid your grieving coworker (avoidance is often viewed by the grieving person as not caring).

During this week after death, your role as a friend, employer, or coworker is to be kind, considerate, and compassionate. Think of the grieving person's needs and desires. Perhaps the shock is just wearing off. Be gentle. Be patient. While the grieving person has much more pain to experience, the pain will lessen with time.

Chapter 6

The First Month and Up to a Year after Death

Providing Emotional Support for Your Friend

A bout three months after my father died, a young man knocked at my door," Jake said. "He introduced himself, saying he had been out of the country for some time, and had recently learned about my dad's death. He offered his condolences, and said that our fathers had worked together many years ago. When he was a child, his family lost everything in a fire. My dad bought him a pair of school shoes. My dad never told anyone about his kindness to this family. Over the course of the year after he died, I heard many wonderful stories about his generosity. The people who shared their reminiscences about him with me were tremendous gifts and helped ease the pain."

Greta's father died three years ago, and her mother died two months ago. Although she is forty-two years old, Greta is an orphan. While she has been grieving her father's death for some time, she now faces the emotional turmoil and grieving tasks that come after a second death. An only child, she also faces the myriad of responsibilities involved in closing her parents' estate, attending to all legal and financial matters. Unfortunately, the timetable of the American legal and taxation systems imposes this burden upon people who are usually incapable of non-emotional decisions. "How am I supposed to handle all the legal issues correctly and logically when I can't even decide what to do with my mom's false teeth?" Greta wailed. The pressing administrative needs may be one reason why folks postpone their grief. They are so busy with paperwork that they have no time for emotion.

Both Jake and Greta are facing the first year of grief after loss. Both will deal with what is called "simple grief," the grief of one loss; and both probably will have what is known as "secondary losses." Greta will also have to address the tasks of "compounded grieving." These terms will be explained later in this chapter.

How Friends Can Recognize Grieving Emotions

Your primary tasks as a friend during this first year after loss are to offer support and comfort, share stories, and listen—again, and again, and again. As your friend moves through the stages of grief, your role and responses will change but your objective is the same: to be a friend. The most valuable gift you can give your friend is your presence. It is far more important than your knowledge or advice. You can acknowledge your friend's sorrow by hugging, holding hands, listening, and crying together.

Your friend will ride an emotional roller coaster during this first year. The grief stages mentioned earlier will continue to cycle, sometimes rapidly, sometimes at a snail's pace. Your awareness of and response to these emotional shifts play an integral part in your friend's grieving process, and in his recovery process.

Let us speak for a moment about the notion of recovery. Some theorists maintain that one eventually recovers from loss, and moves on with one's life. While we believe that people learn to live with loss, we do not believe that one ever fully recovers from the death of a loved one. The reality is that grief never really ends.

The goal is for grief to become a comforting companion, allowing the grieving person to also find joy and meaning in life. This is particularly true in the cases of the death of a child or of a sudden, violent death from an accident, murder, or suicide. In any case, theorists agree that a year must pass before the grieving person can begin to come to terms with the loss. Anniversary dates must be observed: the first Christmas, the first birthday, the anniversary date of the death, and so forth.

The stages and emotions set forth by Westberg and Kübler-Ross are normal grieving reactions. To experience these emotions is healthy, and most professionals strongly encourage grieving people to allow themselves to express them. To suppress them is unhealthy, and can lead to disastrous consequences. Bernie Siegel, M.D., in his landmark book *Love, Medicine & Miracles,*[1] repeatedly cites references linking physical illness to suppressed emotions.

"I grew up in a home where expressing sadness by crying was allowed, but showing anger in any way was not," Greta said. "My parents thought they had left all their financial documents in good order, and in fact they were a mess. I was so angry with them, and so frightened that I might do something illegal. I felt I had no way to express all that anger and fear. Instead of finding a healthy way to deal with my emotions, I became ill—I developed an ulcer and had panic attacks." Fortunately, a friend recognized the symptoms of Greta's suppressed anger, and urged her to talk it out, to exercise it out, and to write it out.

Dan's teenage daughter was killed in a car accident. "I felt tremendous guilt after she died. Why did I let her go out that Saturday night? Why did I let her go alone with her date? Did the fact that I divorced her mother play a part in her death? On and on the questions came, with no answers. Guilt led to depression. I wanted to die too."

Depression is the most common and easily recognized symptom of grief. People who are depressed after death tend to withdraw from past activities; cry, eat, and sleep too little or too much, and sometimes have suicide ideation. A certain amount of these behaviors is to be expected after such a radical change in one's life.

Fear, while not mentioned expressly in the models in this book, is often present in grief. Alma, mentioned in the last chapter, was terrified at night after her husband died. She had rarely spent a night alone in her life. Her husband had always locked the house at night, and now Alma was overwhelmed with fear. She became compulsive about checking the locks five or six times before going to bed. Greta was afraid of all the legal responsibilities her parents left her. We do not always recognize fear in ourselves or in others, and sometimes even when we do, we mask it with other emotions. Anger, in particular, often covers fear. Depression also has fear as one of its components. "I couldn't go into my daughter's room at night. I was so despondent, and worse, I was afraid I'd see her ghost," said Dan.

The belief that one has seen apparitions, heard the deceased person's voice, smelled her cologne, or sensed being touched by the deceased are fairly common. While some, like Dan, may view such experiences as frightening, others find them comforting. Alma told us her husband "came to me one night and said, 'I'm fine, and you will be too.' His visit was so encouraging." Investigating whether or not these sensations are real is beyond the scope of this book; however, your friend probably believes his perception to be true, and your responsibility as a friend is to honor his beliefs.

Worden states that the tasks the grieving person needs to accomplish during this year (or maybe longer) are to face the reality that the person is no longer physically present, to become aware of the roles the deceased played in her life, and to adjust to life without the deceased. He notes that there are often feelings of disorientation, helplessness, and inadequacies. Sometimes the grieving person may be angry and resentful at having to learn new skills, as was Alma's case when the water heater broke.

All of the models discussed maintain that many emotions will occur during the grieving process, and all urge the expression of these feelings. However, there are considerations friends need to make when grief emotions appear to become unhealthy. Some signs to watch for include extended misdirected anger, a major change in physical health status, prolonged depression, long-term insomnia, alcohol or substance abuse, and excessive talk about death.

How to Know When Your Friend Needs Professional Help

Please heed a note of caution as you begin this section. Only qualified mental health and medical practitioners are able to accurately diagnose maladaptive and pathological ideations and behaviors, and must see the patient in order to do so. If you are concerned about your friend, or believe that she is potentially harmful to herself or others, seek professional assistance immediately. The scenarios described in this section are for general information only and are not to be used by nonprofessionals as guidelines for diagnosis.

As mental health practitioners, we strongly advocate consultation with a professional during the grieving process. A competent mental health professional trained in grief work can be invaluable in normalizing the emotions felt by a grieving person, and is trained to recognize symptoms of pathological grief and behaviors. Suicide ideation, for example, is common after some losses; however, a person who has a clear plan and schedule for carrying out a suicide attempt is in need of immediate medical and mental health services.

As noted, depression and anger are normal aspects of the grieving process; however, within the framework of working through grief, if the depression and anger become too severe, mental health services are warranted. "I don't even want to imagine what that first year without my son would have been like without my hospice bereavement counselor," said Mattie. "She literally handed me a lifeline when I was drowning in sorrow." Using talk therapy can be extremely beneficial in helping the grieving person understand, accept, and express emotions in a safe environment.

Sometimes an antidepressant drug may be needed. Only a qualified mental health professional can make this determination, and the medication should be prescribed only by a mental health physician. Some grieving persons desire such medication and ask for it. Greta said she did not seek therapy or medication after her father died. When her mother died, she knew she needed professional help and sought treatment. In addition to talk therapy, she was prescribed an antidepressant, which "helped tremendously."

Others resist medication. "When my sister died, I was a screaming banshee," said Flora. "I was so angry, and so scared. I alternately cried and yelled at my husband, my children, the cashier in the grocery store. My husband begged me to take medication. I said, 'No, I need to feel this pain.' However, I finally consulted my family doctor, who prescribed an anti-depressant. It calmed me right down, but then I was a zombie. I was numb. When I stopped taking it several months later, the pain was still there. I still had to do my grief work. I had only prolonged beginning the process. I should have sought help from a mental health practitioner, not a general practitioner."

In conclusion, we strongly advocate the use of mental health services during the grieving process. However, the task of suggesting such services is often a difficult one for friends. Sometimes it is easier to recommend that your friend speak with a spiritual advisor. An advisor will, in turn, steer the grieving person toward a professional mental health practitioner. You might gently say, "I think it would be helpful if you could talk to an objective person about your feelings. Could I help you look for somebody?" If the answer is no, keep trying. Eventually the grieving person may take your suggestion.

If the answer is yes, there are several ways to locate a competent professional. If your friend's family utilized hospice services for the deceased, the hospice organization usually offers bereavement services for family members for a year after the death of a loved one. Your local hospice organization may have a staff person who sees clients even if they were not family members of a former hospice patient. If your hospice organization does not see nonhospice family members, a staff person can recommend several therapists in your area who specialize in grief issues. Organizations such as the National Association of Social Workers, American Psychological Association, American Psychiatric Association, National Alliance for Mental Illnesses, and others keep a roster of professionals in your area. Also, most religious organizations have counseling centers with mental health professionals who are trained in grief work. Finally, your area mental health center either has a grief professional on staff or can make recommendations.

Secondary Losses

Losses never occur at a good time. Death often comes near a favorite holiday, a family member's birthday, a landmark anniversary. The notion that the initial loss of a loved one is revisited during later happy times is called secondary loss. Each year when Helen lovingly fills her mother's ceremonial Passover dishes, she remembers the tragedy of her parents' deaths. Keith's mother, who loved Elvis Presley, traditionally began the Christmas season by playing Elvis's Christmas album. "The first year after Mom died, I couldn't bring myself to play that disc," Keith said. Martha's daughter died two days before her sixteenth birthday. "Forever, those two dates will be linked in bittersweet memory for me," Martha said.

Secondary loss is perceived as double grief. First, the death of the person is grieved, while the absence of the person during a specific event is also grieved. Sometimes, the grief is so strong as to overshadow joyous occasions. Deb's father died on her nephew's sixteenth birthday, and her mother and brother-in-law shared the same birthday. Although her family continues to make these days special for the living, they will forever be tinged with the memory of loss. A later chapter offers suggestions about rituals and memorials for the deceased during special occasions.

Secondary losses also occur when anything one values is lost. These secondary losses can be powerful. Such losses include a job, a friendship, good health, or possessions. Loss of autonomy or self-esteem also are considered secondary losses, as are the losses of hopes and ideals. For example, soon after his wife died, Warren moved into a nursing home when his own health began to fail. Not only was he grieving the loss of his wife, but the loss of his home, his possessions, and his autonomy.

Compounded Grief

Compounded grieving happens when a person grieves two or more losses simultaneously. Sometimes the losses occur at the same time; sometimes they occur years apart. Whatever the case, the grieving processes are similar, and grief for the losses overlap. Such multiple losses are, unfortunately, fairly common.

The Wilson family's home was destroyed in a recent hurricane. None of its contents, including family photos and valuable antiques, could be salvaged. The old family dog drowned in the storm. The day after the hurricane, Richard Wilson's mother, who lived in a nearby nursing home, had a stroke and died. This family grieved multiple losses simultaneously. While it may appear that a hierarchy of grief should exist in compounded grieving (i.e., Mrs. Wilson should be grieved far more than the dog), such may not be the case. Grief is grief. Sometimes it is impossible to say which loss is the greatest at any one given moment.

Compounded grieving creates compounded emotional stress as well. For example, Mr. Wilson simultaneously may be in an anger stage about the loss of his property, a depression stage about the loss of his mother, and a denial stage about the loss of his dog. It is extremely difficult to work through the grieving process when emotions exist concurrently.

Sometimes loss of a loved one opens old, deep wounds, even when we think those old wounds have healed. Sometimes there is grief for both the loss of tangibles and intangibles. As a small child, an uncle repeatedly sexually abused Amanda. Her grandfather discovered the crime and helped bring the perpetrator to justice. Amanda underwent extensive therapy and believed she had "worked through" her issues and had allowed herself to grieve the loss of her childhood innocence. When her grandfather died, she found herself grieving the losses of her childhood once again, in addition to grieving the death of her grandfather.

Deb has found in her practice that, although clients usually enter therapy to address an immediate loss, they have unresolved grief issues that sometimes date back years. Regardless of the issue the client may overtly bring to therapy, grief is usually an underlying issue. There appears to be an overwhelming sadness that engulfs much of the American population today.

What You Should Do to Offer Emotional Support during the First Year after Death

Denise Anderson,[2] in an article in *Thanatos,* describes grief as a sacred, healing time. Although there are overwhelming emotions of pain and anger, there is usually an internal strength that carries people through this walk. This journey usually makes people stronger and emotionally richer. Your responsibility is to walk with your friend. While you can never feel her feelings, you can be a tremendous support and comfort.

Understand that your friend is no longer the same person you have known, and probably will not be for years. He has been profoundly changed by his experience with death. His life will never be the same again. "When my daughter died, a gigantic, black crater was created in my life. Nothing can ever fill that gaping, terrifying hole. I don't even want anything to fill it. My friends tried, and I pushed them away. The loss was too new, too raw," explained Dan.

Allow your friend to feel and express emotions. Do not place value judgments on your friend's emotions. Emotions are not right or wrong. They simply are. Listen to your friend. No matter how many times she needs to repeat the same story about her loved one, listen as if you have never heard it before. Allow her to cry, to scream and rant, to laugh, and to be silent.

Allow your friend to be indecisive and forgetful. She may accept your invitation to dinner next Saturday, fully intending to attend. Thirty minutes beforehand, she may call you and say, "I can't come. I can't drag myself out of the house." She may not call or show up at all, because she has forgotten you even extended the invitation. Your dinner party is not her priority. Her grief is her only priority.

She may forget your birthday for the first time in thirty years. She may be angry with you for even having a birthday this year. How dare you celebrate a birthday when her sister will never celebrate another? Let it go.

Reminisce with your friend, when he chooses to do so. Do not be afraid to say the deceased person's name. Laughter truly can be wonderful medicine. "Remember the time when . . ." can bring such joy amidst such sorrow. Keith's mother grew up during the Great Depression. As a result, she never threw anything away because "you never know when you may need it." When Keith and his wife cleaned out his mom's house, they found themselves laughing and telling stories about some of the odd items she saved. For example, they found a drawer in the kitchen containing more than three hundred bread ties!

Allow your friend to talk about, and cry about, how much she misses her loved one. Nora, mentioned in the last chapter, had a daily ritual with her husband. When he became too ill to read the newspaper, she sat beside his bed and read it to him. "He particularly loved the comics. Now, when I read the comics, I want so much to share a really funny one with him, and I can't. I miss him so much."

Give your friend permission to be angry, even with you. Do not be shocked by anything your friend may say in anger. He may mean what he says at the moment, but may not the next. Your friend may express anger at his loved one for dying, at the medical profession for letting her die, at himself for not preventing death, or at God for taking her. In her wonderful novel *Christy,* Catherine Marshall[3] says, "those who've never rebelled against God or at some point in their lives shaken their fists in the face of heaven, have never encountered God at all." It is permissible to be angry with God. God can take it.

Allow your friend the freedom of not showing emotion. Remember that grief has no timetable, and it is a misconception to think that a relatively short grieving period means the deceased is not loved.

Finally, educate yourself and your friend on the grieving process. The more you both understand about emotions during this time, the better your relationship will be. Knowing about and recognizing grief stages and processes do not change the feelings, but do help to normalize them. See the suggested reading list at the back of this book or consult your local bookseller.

What You Should Not Do in Offering Emotional Support during the First Year after Death

Do not use the word *should,* as in "you should be feeling . . ." or "you should be doing . . ." There are no "shoulds" in grief work. Folks grieve in their own way, at their own pace. While you may encourage certain behaviors, you cannot dictate what your friend needs to do or not to do.

Do not concentrate on your friend's feelings about her loved one. Concentrate on her feelings about herself. Grief can appear extremely selfish. People who are grieving are self-absorbed and self-focused. This is not bad or wrong, it simply is the way one copes with so much pain.

Do not tell your friend how well she is doing or how strong she is. Behaviors that you may perceive outwardly may not be at all what she is feeling inside. Remember that you do not always know the truth.

Do not be afraid to say what's in your heart. Saying "I'm sorry" in whatever way is natural for you is the best way to communicate your feelings about your friend's loss.

Do not force your friend to talk when he chooses not to discuss his loss. Sometimes there is healing in silence. On the contrary, be aware of when your friend may be in denial and needs to talk.

Do not expect your friend to be aware of your life issues. If she has been your source of strength and your sounding board, it is your turn to be hers. Ask if she is up to the task of hearing your stories. If she is not, find someone else in whom you can confide. Even if she says she is capable of listening to you, she may not really be able to do so. If you find that in the middle of your story she begins telling hers, she is not really hearing you. Do not get angry. Simply stop your story and take it up with another friend.

Ultimately, you need to remember that each person's loss is unique. Sometimes, grief does not appear overtly until after the shock has worn off, sometimes months after the loss. Remember that your friend will never get over it and will never again be her old self; however, with successful grief work, she will survive and be okay.

Chapter 7

The First Month and Up to a Year after Death

Providing Physical Support for Your Friend

W hile the emotional support your friend needs goes hand in hand with the physical support she needs during the first year after loss, we found that separating the two ideas into two chapters makes it simpler to explain your tasks as a friend. This physical support is particularly needed during the first year after a death. Remember that, while your friend must carry on with the day-to-day routines and responsibilities of life, grieving emotions may cloud judgment or preclude your friend's ability to think rationally. Your assistance with day-to-day tasks and some of the necessary responsibilities after someone dies are crucial in assisting in her recovery work.

Household Needs

By now, all the food provided for your grieving friend during the initial time period after death is gone or is unwanted. Preparing a dish for him that is different from all the funeral food would be thoughtful. Remember to bring it in a nonreturnable container.

Errands may need to be run, but your friend may not have the energy to do so (or she may not remember tasks that need to be accomplished). For example, the dog may be due for a checkup. You could volunteer to make the appointment and take him.

Driving may be difficult for a while after a death. Grieving people often are distractible, and driving could be dangerous. Driving at night is particularly difficult, especially if your friend is not accustomed to doing so. Offer to drive him to appointments, events, and religious ceremonies.

The chores that friends tackled earlier need to be accomplished again, some repeatedly. For example, an elderly friend may need someone to do yard work or cleaning. You can either volunteer to do these tasks, commit with a group of friends to do them together, or hire someone to do them for a while.

Be aware of limitations your friend may have regarding household needs. An elderly widow we know attempted to climb a ladder, intent on pruning a small tree. She fell from the ladder and fractured her arm.

Sometimes it is not the large tasks that are daunting for your friend, but the small ones. Alma's husband always opened jars for her because her arthritis made doing so painful. When you visit, ask if such small chores are needed. Note that she may not be able to remember what she needs at the moment. Suggest that she keep a list so that you can help when you make regular visits.

If you know that certain chores were the responsibility of the deceased, offer to do them or arrange to have them done. If your friend is willing, you might even offer to teach him to do these chores. For example, many elderly couples have clearly defined roles and the person left behind has no idea how to accomplish certain tasks. One elderly man we know had no idea how to turn on a washing machine or operate an electric can opener because his wife always did those chores.

Your friend's inability to attend to certain tasks actually may be life-threatening. After Lynn's husband died, lights flickered in her house and her air conditioner stopped working. Fortunately, a friend realized she had a wiring problem and called an electrician who repaired a short in the wiring, thus eliminating a potential fire risk.

Poor nutrition and illness may result from the inability or lack of desire to prepare healthy meals. Another concern is contaminated foods. Some elderly people lose their ability to smell spoiled foods as well as their eyesight to check expiration dates on containers. Those with Great Depression mentality, which we discussed in an earlier chapter, may be unwilling to throw out spoiled food or food that has been in the freezer too long. Of course you can continue to prepare meals, but it would be helpful if you can convince your friend to allow you to teach him some kitchen and shopping basics. If this is not feasible, he may be eligible for home-delivered meals services such as meals-on-wheels through your local senior center.

Elderly people living alone are particularly vulnerable to theft and con artists. Someone suddenly living alone (perhaps for the first time in her life) might suffer panic attacks at night. You might install additional locks for her, and teach her safe ways to answer her door and telephone. You also could set up a telephone chain so friends take turns calling her each evening and morning. Some senior centers offer a daily check-in service. You might give your friend permission to telephone you in the middle of the night if she becomes frightened or just awakens and needs to talk.

Most professionals recommend making as few changes as possible after the death of a loved one; however, there are times when this is not possible. If your friend needs to move, obviously you and others should pitch in to orchestrate the move for him. Keep in mind that if the move is to an assisted living facility or nursing home, visits will be even more appreciated.

Facing Financial Concerns

One of the primary tasks those who are grieving must address is dealing with financial matters. Many folks are not financially prepared for death, and many do not leave instructions or adequate information about monetary issues. Survivors must cope with the daunting chores of changing or closing financial matters, often a stressful responsibility.

Death can be expensive. As noted in previous chapters, mortuaries charge for each service rendered. Reputable mortuaries provide an itemized statement of charges. If your friend does not receive such a statement, you might suggest that he request one. There are costs related to death in addition to mortuary charges. Most newspapers charge per column inch for obituaries. County courts charge for death certificates. If an autopsy is performed, survivors sometimes pay for it. Grave lots can be expensive, as can grave markers or headstones. Clergy and musicians who perform funeral or memorial services are customarily paid. While prepaying death expenses is becoming more the norm in America, many folks do not think so far in advance. This is particularly true if the death is sudden or of a young person.

Unexpected costs are incurred throughout the first year after death. Attorney and accountant fees sometimes must be paid in advance of estate settlement. Your friend may lose income by being absent from work while handling financial matters or from stress-related illness. Some medical expenses incurred prior to death may not be covered by insurance or, even worse, there may have been no insurance, and medical costs are staggering.

If the household has been a two-income one, obviously there is the financial loss of one partner's paycheck. Any sudden change in income is stressful, but losing income from death is additionally so, regardless of your friend's relationship to the deceased.

Lynn, mentioned in chapter 4, was left with two young children after her husband died suddenly of an aneurysm. Both professionals in their mid-thirties, they had not given much thought to the financial aspects of death. Although he carried a small life insurance policy through his work, her husband had little disposable savings. After his death, Lynn found herself a single parent with a single income, trying to pay the mortgage and other expenses alone.

Dana and Tara, sisters in their forties, unfortunately faced a fairly typical situation for adult children. Their father died after a lengthy illness three years ago. Shortly after he died, they placed their mother in a nursing home due to her rapidly declining health. Their father had always handled the finances, and their mother knew little about them. A man of great pride, he had always kept any financial difficulties from his wife and daughters. However, the sisters knew that both parents had Medicare coverage, a secondary insurance policy, and small life insurance policies. They also knew that their parents had wills, leaving all real estate and possessions to them equally.

When the sisters sorted out their parents' finances, they learned that their parents were deeply in debt, so much so that they had been buying medications and paying utility bills with credit cards. The only alternative the sisters had was to sell their parents' home to pay off creditors and to pay for their mother's stay at the nursing home.

While they were still grieving the death of their father, they found themselves also grieving the loss of their mother's health and the loss of their childhood home. They were also faced with the monumental tasks of working with attorneys, the clerk of court, nursing home administrators, accountants, real estate brokers, the Social Security Administration, and the Internal Revenue Service.

Since their mother was moving from the family home, it had to be readied for sale. The sisters had to make decisions regarding the dividing of household items far too quickly. A friend of their mother's appeared to come to the rescue, helping them sort through fifty years' worth of their parents belongings, cleaning house with them, and preparing for an estate sale. In actuality, while the sisters were still in shock, they gave this friend many possessions that they later regretted losing.

If you are a friend of someone who is grieving and coping with administrative tasks simultaneously, be careful about taking articles offered to you. Even if you and your friend are certain that a particular item was meant for you, do not take it right away unless it is specifically stated in the will that you are to have it.

Many of Dana and Tara's friends attended the estate sale. Some months later, Dana noticed one of her mother's favorite dishes in a friend's cupboard. Dana asked how the friend came to have the dish. "It was in the estate sale. I bought it from you. Don't you remember?" Dana was horrified to think that this dish, and many others, probably went into the wrong box, ending up in the sale, as she and Tara, still in shock, were sorting household items. Dana replied, "We didn't mean to sell that dish. Could I buy it back?" Fortunately, Dana's friend was understanding, and returned it to her, refusing reimbursement.

Although Dana and Tara opened the estate sale to the public, they felt as if people pawing through their parents' belongings were vultures. When a man asked the price of a tool, Tara replied that it was one dollar. "Not worth it!" the man snorted, tossing it back into a box. Tara flew into a rage, screaming, "Maybe not to you, but it was to my dead father!" A friend who was helping with the sale took Tara away for a cup of tea while she dealt with her anger.

Sometimes your grieving friend might solicit your assistance and advice in financial concerns. Unless you are an expert in a given financial field, the best practice is to give no advice; however, you can provide assistance in helping your friend to find the proper person to answer questions.

Approaching a grieving friend about his financial matters demands considerable tact. Doing so while your friend is reeling from loss seems even worse. The time may come, however, when you feel you need to step in. For example, if you find stacks of unopened mail on the table, it is a fairly good indication that your friend is not coping with the financial aspects of death. You might say, "Let me help you sort this mail. We can throw out the junk and prioritize the important pieces."

Offering your friend monetary assistance may be exactly what she needs, but it probably will be difficult for you to tactfully make the suggestion and even more difficult for your friend to accept. Again, this conversation depends on your relationship with her. Unless you are really sure about your friend's financial situation, do not offer a loan. Doing so adds the increased burden of worrying about paying the money back later. It is better to give an outright gift of money.

If you are uncomfortable approaching this subject with your friend, you could ask her minister or rabbi to act as an emissary, giving money anonymously through him. You also could give small amounts in other ways, such as filling her gas tank when you are out together, leaving groceries for her, or paying other incidental expenses.

Sorting through Belongings and Memorabilia

Of all the tasks to be accomplished after someone dies, sorting through personal belongings is probably the most difficult. Some folks are anxious to do it right away, some wait until much later, and some cannot ever face this chore. Just as with the emotional aspects of grieving, there are no rights or wrongs in the timing of sorting through belongings, unless there are legal restrictions, monetary concerns, or other time-limited requirements.

For some survivors, the process of sorting through personal belongings is a private task, and they desire no assistance. Usually, doing so brings up many emotions, some of which your friend may not anticipate. If your friend tells you she plans to tackle this chore alone, offer to be available if she needs to talk during the process or afterward. You might also suggest, if your relationship allows, that she discuss her decisions regarding the disposition of items with you or someone who has knowledge of such matters so that she does not make rash decisions. For example, Tara, mentioned above, wanted to send her father's wool suits to hurricane victims in Central America. While this was a noble thought, it was an impractical one.

If your friend requests your presence while she sorts, be prepared for a potentially lengthy process. Accomplishing this task may take quite a while, with decisions being made, then rethought. Also, be prepared to allow your friend time to reminisce, to tell stories, to laugh, and to cry.

One of the most difficult sorting tasks for many folks is the sorting of photographs, videos, and letters. For some, this chore is daunting, but for others, it is comforting. After her father's death, Dana could not bear to look at photos of him. Her sister Tara, on the contrary, created shrines covered in his pictures in her home. Your friend may want you to be there as she sorts through photos and memorabilia. Again, be prepared for this to take time, and be prepared to laugh and cry with your friend.

Help your friend not to make foolish mistakes regarding the disposition of items. If there is a question of monetary value about an article, suggest appraisal by a qualified appraiser. Also, be aware that there are tax laws regarding estate items, and you should recommend that your friend consult an attorney and accountant before making decisions about valuable items.

Your friend may ask you to act as an intermediary while she and other family members go through belongings. The possibilities of family conflict are tremendous during this time. Conflict often occurs even when possessions have little or no monetary value, but intense personal value. We know two brothers who fought over the plastic container that held their mother's Christmas fudge each year!

Be careful if you agree to be present when items are divided among your friend and others. Do not find yourself caught up in family squabbles. As noted in the previous section, do not walk away with items that really are not meant for you. If you do take items, make a list of what you took, make a copy, give one to your friend, and keep a copy in case there is ever any question regarding what you have. Some time after you have received articles, ask your friend if she has reconsidered her gifts to you, and offer to return any item she has regretted giving you. You may even want to ask about this again a year or so later.

Considerations for Employers and Coworkers

When a person loses someone they love, his life is forever changed. Regardless of how well he works through the grieving process, there is now a hole in the world that the deceased person filled. As we suggested in an earlier chapter, recovery from loss does not happen quickly, and people do not get back to normal. Normal, for many, is gone forever.

This change manifests itself in the workplace. A frantic office deadline that may have been vitally important six months ago means nothing today. Planning a supervisor's birthday party has no meaning when the deceased will never again celebrate a birthday. Seeing a photograph on a coworker's desk of his child may be extremely painful for someone who is grieving the loss of her own child.

Some days will be better than others. For some period of time, your coworker may seem to cope fairly well, and then he might experience a setback. Tuesdays may be particularly bad if his loved one died on a Tuesday. There may be dates unknown to you that are painful for him, and he may irrationally expect you to know about them.

During this first year, your coworker may take a greater number of sick days than he previously took. Grief stress frequently manifests itself in many physical illnesses, from colds to heart disease. He may be more tired and irritable at work than usual, due to sadness, anger, and lack of sleep. He may be forgetful and unable to concentrate. He may need to take a number of personal or vacation days to attend to estate matters.

On the contrary, work may be the one place where your coworker can get away from her emotions and estate responsibilities.

She may appear to be almost too cheerful. She also may be in denial. Whatever the reason, your job is not to be judgmental about the way she should behave or execute her duties at work.

As a supervisor, you can recommend counseling if you think your employee needs support; however, he may be resistant to this suggestion. If so, let it go unless his job performance is seriously jeopardized. Others are probably telling him the same thing, and eventually he may take the advice.

Society has a tendency to recommend medication as a panacea for everything, including grief. As a coworker or employer, you do not have the right or expertise (unless you are a mental health or medical professional) to make such a suggestion. As we noted earlier, while medications may be helpful in reducing some symptoms for a while, they do not cure grief.

What to do to support your friend or coworker physically during the first year

If needed, continue to use lists found in other chapters. Remember that this commitment is for at least one year. Consider the following as well:

- ❧ Note in your own calendar special days that may be important to your friend (such as birthday, anniversary, death day) and visit, call, or send a note on these days.
- ❧ Bring food occasionally. Take your friend out for a meal if she will go.
- ❧ Continue to offer your services around the house for chores.
- ❧ Run errands.
- ❧ Drive your friend if driving is difficult.
- ❧ Teach your friend new skills for doing tasks that had been the responsibility of the deceased.
- ❧ Make sure your friend is safe in her home.
- ❧ Connect him to community services that may be helpful (i.e. meals-on-wheels).

~ Offer financial support, if needed, either anonymously or in person.

~ Support your friend through the disposal of property process.

~ Give your friend picture frames or scrapbooks for photos.

~ Find appropriate professionals to help your friend with appraisals, financial, and legal matters.

~ Offer support at work by helping with your coworker's usual tasks.

What not to do during the first year

~ Do not neglect your friend. Although he may not appear to want or need your help, don't give up on him. Keep supporting him.

~ Do not give financial or estate advice you are not qualified to give.

~ Do not take articles unless you are absolutely sure you are meant to have them (i.e., they are expressly mentioned in the will). Even then, check back with your friend periodically to remind him you have certain items, and ask if he has reconsidered giving them to you. If the answer is yes, give them back graciously.

~ Do not get in the middle of family feuds regarding the disposition of property.

Chapter 8

Special Considerations

Certain illnesses and circumstances surrounding death require special considerations by friends and coworkers of those grieving. While the stages of grief are the same, and most of the needs noted in other chapters are applicable, particular issues may need to be addressed and unique comforts given.

Alzheimer's Disease

Alzheimer's disease is the most common form of dementia, affecting people of all ages, races, religions, economic status, and ethnicity. Its course is unpredictable. The patient has days of lucidity when a plateau is reached, and days of total confusion.

Sue's mother began her descent into Alzheimer's disease (AD) slowly. At first, she got lost going to familiar places. She wrote notes to herself constantly, including listing her sisters' names. She became suspicious of people, was less spontaneous, and progressively lost interest in former activities. She began to hide possessions, particularly dinner forks and shoes. Later, she could no longer recognize friends and family. Near the end of her life she stopped eating and remained in bed in a fetal position.

As the illness progresses, caregivers of AD patients find their experience also to be progressively difficult. They have most (if not all) of the anticipatory grieving emotions during the process of the illness. They may feel angry, sad, guilty ("I want my life back, and I feel guilty about wanting it when she's so sick."), discouraged, irritable, or exhausted ("I can't get any sleep. She wanders all night."). Folks who have not experienced caring for a person with AD cannot understand how over-whelming this caregiving job is. Caregivers often feel alone and isolated in their roles.

Unfortunately, one of the by-products of caregiving for an AD patient is that the caregiver loses contact with friends and outside activities. Both friends and other family members may withdraw from the caregiver. Sometimes this withdrawal initiates from respect for the caregiver's time and energy. Sometimes it stems from a lack of understanding: "She must be so busy; she doesn't want to talk to me." The caregiver may initiate the withdrawal because she simply does not have time to focus on anyone except the patient.

Because AD is such a slow, progressive illness, anticipatory grieving can last for years. Also, the grieving needs of the care-giver may be stronger before death than afterward, and support from friends is vital during this time. Be aware, also, that after los-ing her patient to death from AD, the caregiver may experience a tremendous void in her life, as well as a loss of direction and meaning. She still must deal with grief after death. Those same grieving stages that occurred before death will reappear. They may be couched in a different framework, but they still must be addressed. Your friend needs you during both phases of her grief.

What to do for a friend who copes with Alzheimer's disease

❧ Offer to stay with the person with AD so your friend can get out and do something for herself. If she cannot think of any activities, suggest a walk, a movie, or a religious ceremony.

❧ Prepare a meal. Try to organize a group of supporters so that a meal or two can be delivered each week. Make large portions so some can be frozen for another meal.

❧ Offer to feed the person with AD.

❧ Clean the house, do laundry, change linens, wash windows. Ask your friend if there is a particular task that needs addressing.

❧ Run errands.

❧ Pay for occasional respite stays in an adult care center.

❧ Transport the patient to appointments or to an adult care center (if used).

❧ Help install special locks on doors.

❧ Order identification bracelets.

❧ Provide gift certificates to encourage self-care for your friend. Suggestions include certificates for a massage, manicure, pedicure, or hairdresser. Then be willing to sit with the person with AD while your friend is out.

❧ Call if you cannot visit regularly.

❧ When you do visit, do not overextend your time, particularly if the patient is having a difficult day.

❧ Send inspirational cards or notes saying "I'm thinking about you."

❧ Encourage your friend to join a support group. Most cities have caregivers' support groups.

❧ Encourage journal writing.

❧ Allow your friend to vent, to express emotions, concerns, and frustrations.

❧ Help her cultivate her sense of humor. Create opportunities to laugh.

❧ Be nonjudgmental. Your friend is doing the best she can. Tell her so.

AIDS

While there are similarities in grief with all long-term illnesses, AIDS deserves a special mention because of a concept called "disenfranchised grief." Disenfranchised grief occurs when the illness or death of a loved one is not acknowledged or socially accepted. Those who grieve losing someone to AIDS are sometimes denied the opportunity to openly express their feelings and be emotionally supported by friends and family.

The social stigma attached to AIDS, unfortunately, has not lessened very much over the years since AIDS was discovered and named. Society still associates AIDS with risk-taking behaviors, so those who contract it, and their caregivers, often are ostracized. (Interestingly, most of the people we know who have AIDS contracted it from someone whom they believed was a monogamous sexual partner with no known drug habits.) Fear still plays a large part in how people living with AIDS are treated. We have spoken with nurses who refused to care for patients with AIDS, and with family members who were afraid to visit because they might "catch it."

Peggy said that her son, who was HIV positive, developed cancer, which later was the actual cause of his death. "I was so relieved that he got cancer, because I didn't have to tell anyone he also had HIV." Peggy stated that she believed people were far more sympathetic to her grief with a diagnosis of cancer than they would have been with a diagnosis of AIDS.

AIDS, like Alzheimer's disease, is insidious in its progression. We have known persons who had brain damage from the illness and could not communicate verbally. We also have known people who have died from this illness with their faculties intact. In any case, the illness can move quickly or slowly, and can create tremendous anticipatory grief for both the person with AIDS and his caregiver.

Insightful therapist Carl Rogers[1] coined the phrase "unconditional positive regard." Rogers meant that we should hold others in the highest possible regard without demands or stipulations. It means exercising caring without passing judgment. Perhaps with no other population does this concept mean so much as it does with people living with AIDS.

What to do for a friend who copes with AIDS
The list outlined above for Alzheimer's disease also can be used here. Follow these suggestions as well:

- ❧ Be aware of your own feelings about AIDS and people living with it. If you are not sincere in your concern and actions, or are afraid, the people you are trying to help will know it immediately.
- ❧ Hug the patient and the caregiver. Your willingness to touch people living with AIDS speaks of your caring far more clearly than any words ever could.
- ❧ Assist with paperwork.
- ❧ Assist with research concerning legal rights of partners, if the relationship is a nontraditional one.
- ❧ Assist with medication administration (if you feel qualified).
- ❧ Take the patient for an outing, if he feels up to it.
- ❧ If there are children, offer to baby-sit so the caregiver or the patient can get out for a while.
- ❧ Assist with birthday parties and holidays.
- ❧ Provide emotional support. Allow the caregiver and the patient an opportunity to express emotions.
- ❧ Listen.

After a death, the caregiver needs all the support listed above and in other chapters, but pay special attention to the following:

- ❧ Enable the survivor to tell his story.
- ❧ Understand that survivors of someone who has died from AIDS may have strong emotional outpourings, particularly anger, fear, guilt, and shame. Allow your friend to express those emotions. Remember that emotions are not right or wrong. They simply are.

✺ Your friend may have feelings of abandonment, both by
the deceased person and by friends and family who, for
whatever reason, were not present during the illness and
death. Allow your friend to express those feelings.

✺ Be patient. Remember that grief has peaks and valleys,
and is a roller coaster. Give your friend time and space.

✺ Remember birthdays, anniversaries, holidays, and death
days. Perhaps you and other friends and family
members could assist in planning and carrying out a
special ritual or memorial service on these days.

What not to do for a friend who copes with AIDS

✺ Do not avoid the grieving person.

✺ Do not be judgmental.

✺ Do not avoid mentioning the name of the deceased.

✺ Do not get involved with family conflicts.

✺ Do not load up your friend with "shoulds." You have no
right to tell her what she needs to, or should, do or not do.

Abortion

Regardless of how or why the decision is made for an abortion, it is usually not made lightly and there is always the loss
of a child. Grief may or may not be apparent immediately after
the abortion; sometimes it appears years after the event.
Grieving the loss of a child through abortion may be lonely,
particularly if the mother does not share the experience with
others or if she is in conflict with family members about her
decision. She may have no one with whom she feels she can
share her anguish.

If you have a friend who is contemplating an abortion, listen
to her while she struggles with her decision. Let her verbalize
problems associated with this decision and enable her to discuss
available alternatives. Suggest counseling by a professional, if
appropriate. Do not make the decision for her.

If your friend has completed the abortion and needs to talk, be a good listener. Allow her to mourn, to share her sadness. Do not be judgmental or discuss your own values and beliefs. If you are uncomfortable listening, be honest. Encourage your friend to seek counseling services from a professional therapist, minister, or rabbi.

Remember that grief from an abortion can last for years, even though that grief can be hidden for a time. Ten years after an abortion, Pamela was happily married and anticipating the arrival of children. For many years, she was unable to conceive, and her suppressed guilt engulfed her. "I went into a state of depression and felt I was a failure. I believed I had given up my opportunity to have a healthy child." Pamela finally did bear a child. She was elated, "but my first thought when I saw him was for the child I had aborted."

Your responsibility as a friend to someone who grieves loss through abortion is to listen. Do not be judgmental.

Miscarriage

According to the National Institute of Child Health and Human Development, National Institutes of Health Web site, about 15 percent of all pregnancies end in miscarriages.[2] Unfortunately, society does not attend nearly well enough to those grieving such deaths. Some of the most callous comments we have heard in our work have come from well-meaning people to those suffering loss from miscarriages. "You didn't really know this child because it wasn't born yet." "You can have others." "You should try to get pregnant again right away." "At least you have other children." What awful, insensitive statements!

Most often, in an anticipated pregnancy, parents begin to bond with a baby the minute the pregnancy is confirmed. This bonding becomes stronger as gestation progresses. When a miscarriage occurs, grief can be overwhelming. All the stages of grief appear. The mother may also feel that she is a failure because she was unable to bring the baby to term.

Marcy miscarried her first child in August many years ago. Every August thereafter she has experienced depression, anger, sadness, and guilt over the life that might have been. Her feelings of loss never leave her.

Stillbirth

In a stillbirth, like a miscarriage, a life is ended before it has an opportunity to develop. Also, like in a miscarriage, attempts at comforting the grieving parents can be clumsy at best.

The difference between miscarriage and stillbirth is that in a miscarriage the fetus does not come to term, while in stillbirth a body must be cared for. Parents may choose to have a Baptism or memorial service in the hospital chapel. Some parents find a picture or footprint of the baby comforting.

Remember that your friend not only grieves the loss of the child, but all the events in the child's life that will never happen (the first tooth, high school graduation, marriage, children).

If you are a friend to someone grieving a stillbirth or miscarriage, some of the suggestions below may be helpful.

What to do when a friend suffers a miscarriage or stillbirth
- ❧ Attend whatever rituals or services your friend chooses to hold.
- ❧ Plant a memorial tree or bush for the family.
- ❧ Suggest that your friend light a memorial candle on holidays and special days, and participate in the lighting of this candle.
- ❧ Suggest that your friend join a support group, such as Compassionate Friends, an international organization for those grieving the loss of children.
- ❧ Suggest that your friend keep a journal of her grief work.
- ❧ Remember the anniversary date with a card or a call.

Death of a Child at Any Age

While in theory we believe that all grief is equal, we feel that in reality there is no greater grief than the loss of a child, regardless of the age. Whether the child is a newborn infant or twenty-one years old, all the theories we know regarding grief work seem to be invalid or, at best, inadequate. In our experience, families who have children die never appear to reach the closure stages noted by the experts.

Dan, whose daughter was killed in a car accident, told us, "I learned to get through each day in a fog. I became a robot, doing what needed to be done at work, at home. The sharp, searing pain became a dull ache, which never goes away for a moment. Even as I learned to laugh again, I mourned that I could never laugh again with her."

We expect elderly people to die. That is the order of nature. Somehow, the death of a young person disrupts this order. Most of us question the reason for death for anyone: "Why did he have to die of cancer? Of a heart attack?" There are, of course, no answers to these questions, but when they are asked about the death of a young person, the void seems bottomless: "Why so young? Why now?"

Often there is tremendous guilt surrounding the death of a youngster, regardless of the cause of death. The "if onlys" and the "what ifs" are endless. April's daughter left home at sixteen, living on the road, calling home occasionally, and usually coming home for Christmas. At twenty-eight, she was found dead of a heroin overdose. April's anguish was inconsolable. "I wish I could have locked her in her room until she was thirty, keeping her safe. If only I had been more aware of her drug problem . . . if only I had tried to stop her . . . if, if, if." The answer is that there are no answers.

Beth's daughter died at age ten of leukemia. The years of treatments, the false promises of periods of remission, and the final acceptance of the illness took their toll on the whole family. Beth and her husband found themselves grieving the loss of their daughter differently from each other. Beth cried and wailed, while her husband maintained a stoic silence. The loss of a child can bring family members close to each other, or it can rip a family apart. Beth's mother said, "Why did she have to die? Why couldn't it have been me? I'm old and ready to go." Again, there are no answers.

What to do when a friend has a child die

Use any of the suggestions mentioned earlier in this chapter, as well as the following:

- ❧ Listen . . . again and again and again. Your friend needs more than anything to talk about the child. She needs to tell stories about his life and to mourn all the events that will never be.
- ❧ Say the child's name. Doing so validates his life.
- ❧ Remember anniversary dates with a card, a telephone call, or a visit.
- ❧ Honor the child with a memorial gift to a foundation or organization.
- ❧ Create a living memorial by planting a tree, giving books to the local library (or his school library) in his memory, or donating playground equipment to his favorite park.

Suicide

According to Beryl S. Glover,[3] suicide can be one of the most tragic forms of death. It is almost impossible to predict. According to the Centers for Disease Control, in the year 2000 alone, 29,350 lives were lost to suicide in America.[4] Suicide rates are especially high among the elderly, but often are misdiagnosed. Many elderly people suffer from chronic physical illness and cannot tolerate the loss of independence and self-sufficiency. Elder suicide often has been ruled as unintentional drug overdose. Fortunately, medical professionals are becoming more aware of the growing trend of elderly depression and suicide, and are taking measures to help.

Suicide patterns have changed among young people recently, and attempts have risen dramatically. Suicidal adolescents, like suicidal adults, may be deeply depressed, but signs are sometimes difficult to recognize because they may manifest themselves as boredom or physical complaints.

There are many reasons people commit, or attempt to commit, suicide, but that discussion is beyond the scope of this book. However, it is important to note that any suicide attempt or threat should be treated seriously. If you suspect that a friend or coworker plans a suicide attempt, seek professional assistance immediately.

The stigma of this type of death can entail more shock and denial than many other kinds of deaths. Survivors of a suicidal death certainly experience all the stages of grief, but they often have a prolonged period of numbness, so that there appears to be an absence of feeling.

The suicide survivor has the right to feel (or not to feel) any emotion after the death of a loved one. She may feel shame, guilt, or disbelief: "Why didn't he leave me a note?" She may blame herself: "What did I do wrong?" "Could I have prevented it?" She also may feel anger or a sense of relief that the person no longer suffers from mental or physical illness.

Suicide survival can be thought of as another kind of disenfranchised grief, one not generally discussed. This often results in a lack of emotional and social support for the survivor. Fortunately, this stigma is changing, and the pain felt by the survivors is becoming more easily acknowledged.

What to do when a friend has survived a suicide death
 ❧ Encourage your friend to talk about her feelings.
 ❧ Help your friend deal with "unfinished business"
      (i.e., finding a way to say good-bye).
 ❧ Be careful about being judgmental. Avoid clichés.

❦ Allow your friend to cry, scream, or express emotions in any way. Be aware of potentially intense feelings.

❦ Help your friend to laugh and to celebrate the life of the deceased person.

❦ Encourage your friend to join a support group. Most cities have such groups for suicide survivors.

❦ Understand the uniqueness of suicide grief.

Death of a Pet

The death of a pet can be traumatic for both children and adults. Pets love unconditionally. They ask for little in return for affection and companionship. Fortunately, society is beginning to accept the reality of the grief felt when a pet dies.

Deb lived for eighteen years with Merlin, the Magic Cat. He was her constant companion, loving to ride in the car, walk on the beach, and even ride in her boat. When he died, it was as if her best friend had died. Merlin also was special to many of Deb's friends, and some of them were with Deb and Merlin in his final hours. Friends and family brought food and attended a memorial service honoring his life. Merlin was cremated, and Deb's friends helped her scatter his ashes. A friend painted a portrait of him from a photograph. Her employer granted her three days of bereavement leave from work.

Grief over the death of a pet is no different from grief over a person, although the grief varies in intensity from person to person. One can experience all the emotions common to grieving the loss of a person, including anger (particularly if the pet was killed) and guilt ("I should not have left her outside"). It is important to note that each member of a family has a unique relationship with a family pet, and each relationship should be honored, including the variety of emotions that various family members may feel at any one given time.

Children should be involved in any rituals and memory sharing regarding a pet. If the decision is made to euthanize the pet, children should be informed beforehand, so that they can have their special time to say good-bye.

Older adults often have special relationships with their pets, particularly if they live alone with the pet. Sometimes the death of a pet can bring up old feelings regarding the death of a loved one, resulting in compounded grief.

What to do when a friend has a pet die
Certainly, all the suggestions in this book regarding the death of any loved one can apply to the death of a pet. However, below are some special considerations:

❧ Be careful regarding how you express sympathy. Treat the death as you would any other loss. Do not minimize the death in any way. Do not say, "You can get another cat." "I know someone who has a dog just like yours and she just had puppies." "At least you can go out now without worrying about the dog."

❧ Telephone, send a card, or visit.

❧ Offer to frame a special photograph of the pet. A friend who recently lost a pet was given a beautifully framed poem about, and photo of, his cat.

❧ Present your friend with an ornament or statue that symbolizes his relationship with his pet.

The special considerations described in this chapter are not meant to be exhaustive, but we believe the suggestions noted here can be applied to almost any death circumstance.

Chapter 9

Holidays and
Special Events

For fifty-four years, Grace celebrated the first day of each new year with her family gathered around her table, eating black-eyed peas and collards for good luck. On the first New Year's Day after the death of her daughter, Erica, Grace could not bring herself to prepare this special meal. She told her family that she was not cooking anything. Grace's husband said, "Erica would want us to carry on as usual." Grace's son flatly refused to participate: "It's too soon. I would hurt too much, missing her at the table." Grace's daughter-in-law offered to cook the meal for her. Grace's sister suggested that they prepare a different menu. Grace fretted and vacillated about her decision, torn by her own need and those of her family members.

Holiday traditions and rituals can be the most stressful part of the grieving process. Family members and friends are experiencing various stages of grief during these times, often in conflict with each other. Carrying on traditions exactly as they had been carried out for years is comforting for some folks, painful for others.

Again, there are no rights or wrongs in making decisions about holidays; however, it is difficult to meet everyone's needs.

It is important to examine why a tradition or ritual is repeated year after year. "Because we have always done it that way" may not be a good enough reason to continue after the death of a loved one. A break from tradition is not necessarily bad or wrong, and need not be forever. Perhaps changing the ritual for just one year is enough, and then the tradition can return the following year. The Carter family had for fourteen years camped cross-country in the summer. The summer following Mr. Carter's death, the family decided to forego the usual trip because of the painful memories it would evoke. The next summer, however, they reinstated the tradition in memory of Mr. Carter.

On the contrary, there is comfort for some in repeating traditions each year. Each Mother's Day from age fourteen until his mother died, Keith planted a rose in her garden. After her death, he carried on this tradition by donating a rose to a local arboretum. "There is solace for me in giving that rose to a good cause. In some way, my mom lives on in the flowers others now enjoy."

Rituals also have to do with continuity and renewal. The Jewish Passover Seder, commemorating Jewish freedom from Egyptian bondage, also represents God's eternal promises of hope and faith. The traditional readings, prayers, foods, and serving pieces are important components of the holiday. "Each year as I set the table with my mother's traditional dishes, I am reminded not only of her love for her faith, but of God's love for me," said Dina.

In the Christian faith, Christmas is usually the most stressful of all holidays when one is grieving. All the bright lights, glitter, cheerfulness, and joy seem to mock the feelings of desolation and pain. Grieving persons tend to have low energy, and this lack of energy appears to be exacerbated by such a high-energy time of year. There is often no impetus for shopping, decorating, cooking, and gift giving.

It is difficult for a grieving person to give himself permission to change traditions, particularly when expectations from others run high or when necessity seems to dictate otherwise. Dan, whose daughter died in a car accident, has two younger children. "Although they missed their sister, they still expected Santa to come. I had to put their needs above my own. If I'd had my way, I would have sat in the dark for months." Alma reacted differently to the holiday. "Historically, I spent months shopping for just the right gifts for my family. The Christmas after my husband died, I had no energy for shopping. Instead, I sent a check to his favorite charity in his memory and in honor of my family members. It felt strange and empty to do so, but it was the best I could do."

Lynn, whose husband died suddenly of an aneurysm, said, "I tried to find appropriate Christmas cards that first year, but I couldn't. They all said 'joy' and I didn't feel any joy. I couldn't bring myself to send Christmas cards, particularly to folks far away with whom we only communicated at this time of the year. What was I to say? 'Merry Christmas! My husband is dead.'" Lynn solved this problem by sending spring cards when she felt more able to communicate.

Birthdays and anniversaries also are particularly difficult occasions for grieving people. These days often go unnoticed by friends and coworkers because the dates are unknown to people outside the immediate family. Vivian, mentioned in chapter 5, had an important presentation at work on the date that would have been her fiancé's birthday. She had problems concentrating and was tearful most of the morning. Fortunately, a coworker saw her distress and offered to make the presentation for her.

The anniversary date of a loved one's death is never forgotten by those grieving, but seldom is remembered exactly by friends. Deb learned this lesson the hard way. The father of a good friend died near Memorial Day. While she could not remember the exact date, she did remember the occasion. She telephoned her friend and was told, "I wish you'd called yesterday. I needed to talk on the anniversary date." Now Deb and Sue keep records of death days in their calendars the same way they note birthdays.

American culture is rich in holidays. Regardless of one's spiritual beliefs, there are holidays for celebration and feasting, and holidays for fasting and contemplation. Of course we also have secular holidays that are woven into the thread of the American fabric—Fourth of July, Labor Day, Arbor Day, and so forth. Because it would be overwhelming to attempt to address each holiday in this chapter (and because we might inadvertently omit an important holiday in a particular religion), we will dedicate the remainder of this chapter to suggestions for the three categories of holidays noted above. At the end of this chapter are suggestions for rituals that might be comforting to your friend.

Religious or Spiritual Celebration Days

Examples of religious celebration days include Mardi Gras, Easter Sunday, All Saints Day, Christmas Day, Chanukah, Passover, Rosh Hashanah, and Kwanzaa. As mentioned earlier, celebration holidays often are the most difficult for grieving people because a celebration time almost feels as if the occasion is mocking grief. How can one be joyous when one is in such pain? The truth is, sometimes the pain *is* too great. Celebration holidays evoke strong memories of happier times, and your friend may need to express those memories. Here are some suggestions for you in helping your friend through these events:

- ❧ Give your friend permission to feel and express any emotions he may be having at this time.
- ❧ Do not expect your friend to feel, or behave, in a certain way. Grief is individual.
- ❧ Allow your friend to remember past holidays. Listen to the stories, and laugh and cry with your friend.
- ❧ Help your friend focus on what is really important to her.
- ❧ Help your friend formulate choices.
- ❧ Give your friend permission to examine and then change rituals, if he chooses to do so.

❧ Help your friend undertake changing rituals if he chooses to do so.

❧ If your friend decides to keep old traditions, help with those too.

❧ Often, much preparation is needed prior to a celebration holiday. Help with this preparation: clean, shop, write invitations, decorate, polish silver, cook, etc.

❧ After the holiday, help with cleanup.

❧ Remember that many celebration holidays last for more than one day (Christmas, Kwanzaa, Chanukah, etc.), and your friend may need you to be on duty for several days.

❧ Expect that, regardless of your friend's decision concerning how she will or will not acknowledge a holiday, she will ride a roller coaster of emotion. Be patient and be sensitive to emotions that can change at any moment.

❧ Your friend may want to attend religious services during this time. Offer to attend with him.

❧ Your friend may want to attend a service different from his usual one. Offer to go with him or to transport him if he wants to go alone.

❧ Your friend may want to visit the cemetery or location where ashes were scattered. Go with her. If flowers or some token of remembrance are appropriate, bring them.

❧ If, at a meal or some other occasion during the holiday, a special prayer or reading may be appropriate, ask your friend's permission to express your sentiments. Usually, a grieving person deeply appreciates your remembrance of the deceased.

Religious, Spiritual Fasting, and Contemplation Days

Examples of religious fasting or contemplation days are Ash Wednesday (and all of Lent), Good Friday, All Hallows Eve, and

Yom Kippur. These are days of reflection and humility in most religions and often bring about sadness in the grieving person. One tends to examine behaviors, look at old guilt, and ask the "what if" and "if only" questions. During these times, pain may seem appropriate to your friend. The following are suggestions for helping your friend during these times:

- ❧ Give your friend permission to feel and express any emotions he may be having at this time.
- ❧ Do not expect your friend to feel or behave in a certain way.
- ❧ Allow your friend to remember days past. Listen to the stories and cry with your friend.
- ❧ Expect that, regardless of your friend's decision concerning how she will or will not acknowledge a holiday, she will ride a roller coaster of emotion. Be patient and be sensitive to emotions that can change at any moment.
- ❧ Your friend may want to attend religious services during this time. Offer to attend with him.
- ❧ Your friend may want to visit the cemetery or location where ashes were scattered. Go with her. If flowers or some token of remembrance are appropriate, bring them.
- ❧ If at the fast-breaking meal or some other occasion during the holiday a special prayer or reading may be appropriate, ask your friend's permission to express your sentiments. Usually, a grieving person deeply appreciates your remembrance of the deceased.
- ❧ Ask your friend if he wants your company or if solitude is needed. Honor his request, but make it clear that you are available if he changes his mind.

Secular Holidays

Examples of secular holidays include New Year's Day, Valentine's Day, Mother's Day, Memorial Day, Father's Day, Fourth of July,

Labor Day, and Thanksgiving Day. Almost every American has some memory attached to some of these days, whether they are pleasant or unpleasant memories. They are traditionally days for family gatherings, expressions of love, and fun. How your friend reacts to each depends on his own history and his relationship with the deceased. Listed below are general suggestions for any secular holiday:

- ❧ Ask your friend for information regarding her history of an upcoming holiday.
- ❧ Ask what she plans to do this year and offer to be supportive of her decision.
- ❧ If your friend says she plans to ignore the event, give her choices of alternative activities. For example, if she plans to stay home on Independence Day and you're having a picnic, give her the option of joining you.
- ❧ Allow her to change her mind and show up unexpectedly, or allow her to leave if she attempts to attend and finds the event too painful.

Individual Special Occasions

Examples of individual special occasions include birthdays, anniversaries of marriages, christenings, Baptisms, bar or bat mitzvahs, and death dates. As we mentioned earlier, Sue and Deb note these dates in their calendars for their friends. Honoring these events with your friend may be important to her, particularly in the first few years after a loss.

When remembering the anniversary date of a death, several thoughts bear consideration. It is important to remember that an actual anniversary date may not be the most important part of the memory for your friend. For example, Deb's dad died on Tuesday, July 21. Obviously, July 21 moves through the week over the years, but the Tuesday before the actual date is still more difficult for her than the actual date. For others, the date of the memorial service holds a stronger memory. Again, keep in mind that a personal anniversary may be more than just the calendar date for your friend.

Other nonspecific dates may trigger strong emotions in your friend. For example, if your friend has lost a child, the first day of each school year may be difficult. Prom and graduation time may be painful.

Below are suggestions for individual special occasion dates:

- ❧ As noted, keep these dates in your calendar.
- ❧ Speak to your friend prior to upcoming events and learn what times might be the most difficult for her. Offer your assistance.
- ❧ Speak to your friend on the actual date and be available if you are needed.
- ❧ Be aware of upcoming nonspecific occasions that may trigger a reaction in your friend and be present if you are needed.

Special Considerations in the Workplace

The office Christmas party may not be important to an employee who has recently lost a loved one. Facing the annual Labor Day company picnic and family softball game may be painful for an employee whose child has just died. Thursdays may be just Thursdays to a supervisor, but they are a constant reminder of loss for an employee whose mother died on a Thursday.

Sensitive supervisors keep calendars of important dates in their employees' lives. Doing so allows them to schedule workloads and anticipate needs employees may have regarding those dates.

While we do not recommend that an employer ignore special occasions, we do suggest sensitivity to a grieving employee's needs. The best practice is to ask what the employee needs, understanding that needs and feelings may change.

Rituals for Special Occasions

Each major religion has a guidebook that contains passages of comfort to the grieving person, both initially after loss and for years afterward. Some religions have memorial rituals that are performed on certain dates annually or are part of other rituals within the context of certain holidays. Depending on your friend's beliefs, he may want to utilize these ceremonies as part of his healing process. You can gently remind him to avail himself of his belief's rituals.

There are other times, however, when a ritual may be appropriate that is not part of the traditions of a given religious belief. Even when such tradition is available, your friend may choose to have a private ritual outside of his religious organization. Such times may be birthdays, anniversaries, and death dates.

Today, thousands of other books have suggestions for rituals for honoring the deceased (see recommended reading section), and we believe these books can provide excellent resources. In this section, however, we provide you with the tools for creating rituals, either for or with your friend, to be used whenever it is deemed appropriate.

Rituals generally follow a pattern of invocation, a time for being quiet and meditative, listening, responding, and benediction. Certainly you and your friend can write your own words for rituals, or you can borrow from published prayers, poems, essays, and songs.

Many symbols are used in rituals, and which symbols you choose to employ are entirely up to you. Usually, symbols in some way relate to the occasion being commemorated, to the person being remembered, and to the five senses. You may want to include music and musical instruments, dance, singing, incense, sage, cedar, perfumes or other scents, photographs and art, articles that represent texture, and food for the sense of taste. Some symbols are universal, for example, light, water, fire, air, and earth; some are highly personal, such as seashells, pebbles, photographs, personal effects, and so forth. Whatever and however you conduct the ritual is acceptable, as long as it honors the deceased person and those who remember him.

Sometimes rituals can be adaptations of other, more familiar rituals. For example, the lighting of advent candles or the menorah candles can be accompanied by specific prayers and thoughts of your loved one.

Chapter 10

Death by Catastrophe

Most people remember where they were and what they were doing when a particular major tragedy occurred. Sue remembers exactly what she was wearing when the school principal announced that John Kennedy had been assassinated. Deb knows exactly how she felt when she learned that Martin Luther King Jr. and Mother Teresa were dead. We certainly remember exactly what we were doing on the morning of September 11, 2001. We know that we, along with many other people around the world, continue to grieve the losses we experienced on that day.

This book was begun well before September 11, 2001, and it was born from personal losses that we and people we know experienced. We originally intended to incorporate information about accidental and traumatic death into another context, using the timeline created in previous chapters. In light of recent international events, however, we decided that catastrophic death and loss warrant a separate chapter. To be entirely honest, this has been the most difficult chapter to write in this book.

There are many reasons that this is a difficult chapter, both for the authors and for the reader. First, the emotions from September 11, 2001, are too new, too raw. We as professionals are learning daily about the impact catastrophic events can have. Regarding September 11, it is difficult to sort through grief emotions when one is in the midst of grief.

Never before has grief had so many layers. Individuals who lost family members certainly grieve intensely. Individuals who lost friends and coworkers grieve intensely in a different way. All of New York City, Pennsylvania, Washington, D.C., and northern Virginia grieve at one level—and the rest of the nation and the world grieve at another.

We read in the popular press soon after the events of September 11 that the whole nation could be diagnosed as having experienced a major depressive episode. This certainly may have been true initially after the tragedy. Some professionals also believe that now, some time after September 11, the whole nation could be considered to be suffering from post-traumatic stress disorder. Diagnosing an entire country with a mental illness is not something mental health professionals have ever done before. We are not sure such a diagnosis is accurate, but we do believe that it would be accurate to say many of those close to the tragedy still clearly suffer emotionally from their losses. We also know that those who continue to experience death through war and political unrest both in America and abroad grieve additional losses.

We see our response to the emotional needs of survivors changing daily as new issues surface. While professionals have guidelines to follow based on prior events, nothing could have prepared us for such large-scale grief. Volumes of literature are being produced continually that examine our response to the needs of those in grief. Organizations skilled in large-scale disaster work find themselves challenged by the immensity of the task.

Our intent in this chapter is not to address the organizational response to disaster, trauma, and grief, but our response as individual friends, neighbors, and coworkers. Few of us have the skill for supporting large numbers of people in grief. We can only do what we can within our own small frame of reference. To attempt to do otherwise would be overwhelming.

While still in shock, Deb had a brief moment of lucidity a few hours after the events of September 11 and checked in with her county emergency management director with whom she has worked during several hurricanes. Obviously, emergency procedures were being activated around the country, and Deb's responsibility was to be ready at a moment's notice in her capacity as a mental health professional. Fortunately, her services were not needed in her community during the immediate crisis.

Beginning shortly after the crisis and continuing until today, however, Deb still counsels people who are experiencing grief from the events of September 11. She has had clients who lost friends and family members in New York and Washington, D. C. She has had clients who faced financial losses and bankruptcy because of the disaster, and grieve the loss of homes and jobs. While the grief issues of a nation certainly correspond to the grief issues of an individual, we really can only address grief one person at a time.

As a frame of reference for large-scale disasters, let's review Westberg's model outlined in chapter 1 as it might apply to traumatic or sudden death.

Shock, Denial, and Panic

We almost never seem to be able to make sense of loss and death, especially traumatic death, and particularly immediately after the event occurs. For many of us, the replaying of the World Trade Center crashes on television exacerbated the sense of unreality, making us believe we were watching a science fiction movie, complete with model airplanes and special pyrotechnic effects. Repeatedly watching the tragedy brought a nightmare quality to our senses. As noted in previous chapters, that period of shock and denial after death serves a valuable purpose—it cushions us against being overwhelmed by the immensity of the pain. The feeling of unreality allows us time to ease into the truth of the situation.

Emotions Erupt

The initial sense of shock after trauma often gives way to fear and horror, sometimes with dramatically erupting emotions. Certainly this was the case after September 11 as the nation faced (and continues to face) the potential for additional attacks. For example, many Americans, in panic, rushed to buy gas masks.

Natural disasters also may elicit shock, fear, and horror. After the rash of hurricanes that struck the North Carolina coast in the late 1990s, thousands of dead farm animals floated in rivers and creeks. This gruesome scene is indelibly etched in the memory of those who witnessed this trauma, either in person or on television.

Anger

Anger is very common after a traumatic death. After September 11, many Americans screamed for immediate retaliation. Others directed anger toward the U.S. government, believing that it should have known and protected American soil. In the seeming chaos that reigned immediately after the event, many people lashed out at officials who were probably doing the best they could do under the circumstances.

Illness

It may be some time before we can accurately assess the physical illness toll September 11 has had on the loved ones of those who died that day. Studies are underway to collect and examine data. Based on previous work we have done, we feel sure that research will support a dramatic increase in grief-related illnesses.

Guilt

The media bombarded the American public after September 11 with "if only" human interest stories, stories that told of loved ones who forgot to say "I love you" or "I'm sorry for our spat last night" before the fateful event. Guilt includes components of self-blame, helplessness, and lack of control. We saw clients after September 11 who were suffering from personal losses, simultaneously feeling guilty about their pain during such a large-scale tragedy. As we discussed earlier, forgiveness is an important part of healing grief. We believe that doing so on a national level is just as important as on a personal level.

Depression and Loneliness

As Deb and Sue were glued to news broadcasts during the evening of September 11, they watched Ted Koppel tearfully suggest that folks should telephone family members to say, "I love you." Both of us followed Koppel's advice, speaking with loved ones throughout the crisis. At the moment Koppel made this suggestion, the shock Deb had been feeling all day erupted into her own tears, and turned into depression and loneliness. Certainly these emotions were felt for the people suffering unspeakable losses at that moment, but they also were felt for her own grief over the loss of her parents. She remembers thinking, "I would give anything to be able to talk to my parents right this minute."

Reentry Difficulties

How does one return to normalcy when there is no normalcy in which to return? The mind does not readily accept that someone, or something, is just gone. One second the person you love the most is speaking with you on a cell phone, and the next second he's dead. Such a thought is beyond comprehension. You cannot go to work because the building in which you have worked for many years is a gigantic pile of rubble.

Reentry after a major traumatic event may take longer than reentry from an expected loss. This may be true because the path through the emotions may take longer to navigate—the more traumatic the loss, the longer the period of shock.

Hope

The tremendous outpouring of support from the world after the events of September 11 gave many Americans hope that our losses were not felt in isolation. The memorials and monuments to the lives lost bring comfort to many of those who will grieve for a long time to come.

While we have used September 11 as an example of traumatic and sudden loss, there are many others. For example, murder, accidents, and unexpected heart attack or other illness create similar emotional and physical responses.

Unfortunately, traumatic and sudden losses may necessitate dealing with exceptionally painful situations. Noted below are several such issues:

❧ There may be no body.

❧ Only parts of a body may be recovered, or the body may be unrecognizable or grotesquely disfigured. This situation borders on the macabre and can be the stuff of nightmares for a long time.

❧ For whatever reason, the authorities may not release the body immediately or may perform an autopsy before it is released.

❧ The body may have to be shipped from far away.

❧ The body may not be found until months later.

These situations make the initial stages of shock and denial particularly painful, because there are no visible means for finality. With several of the points noted above, the shock and denial may be coupled with hope. While hope can be affirming of life, it also can delay acceptance of reality.

It may be necessary for your friend to identify her loved one, whether or not she would choose to view the body. If your friend views the body, the memory may be extremely painful. The sense of unreality lingers for quite a while. Insist on accompanying her, at least as far as you are able or as she wishes you to go. Do not let her undertake such a devastating event alone. Certainly, this will be traumatic for you as well, so be sure that you have supports for yourself in place before you go.

On the contrary, viewing the deceased person may be beneficial to your friend. We believe the mind is merciful sometimes and softens the image before us. Amy's parents were killed in a head-on car accident on a rural road. She had to drive several hundred miles to identify both her parents' bodies. She remembers nothing of their injuries, but clearly remembers peacefulness in their faces. Whether or not this was real is not the point. What Amy's mind remembers is important.

As noted in previous chapters, catastrophic loss may bring back other grieving issues called "secondary losses." Also note that in a situation of multiple losses, your friend is experiencing compounded grieving. This was especially true with the many employees of one business who died together on September 11.

Remember that during a traumatic event, more than human lives are lost. Cherished objects also can disappear. For example, how many wedding bands were lost at the site of the World Trade Center?

What you can do for friends and coworkers after traumatic loss

❧ During the initial shock phase, suggest that your friend take "media holidays" even if she turns off the television for just a few minutes during each break. In her work with disasters, Deb has found that people tend to develop sensory overload when exposed to too much information. During fast-breaking news, it becomes impossible to differentiate between important updates and commercials. If information is really important, it will be repeated shortly. A few quiet minutes will help your friend collect her thoughts and feelings as well.

❧ Assist your friend in gathering information about his loved one. Ensure that your friend has organized documentation (such as photographs, social security number, birth date, driver's license number, etc.) that may be needed to verify information about the deceased person.

❧ Help your friend access relief services and complete documentation, such as registering with the American Red Cross, Federal Emergency Management Agency and local relief agencies, as appropriate.

❧ If you are qualified and feel comfortable doing so, help your friend with financial and legal matters that will arise. If you are not qualified, assist your friend in finding a reputable person who can help.

❧ Your friend may be approached by the media for interviews. Be supportive of your friend's decision about speaking with the media. If your friend chooses to be interviewed, help in deciding what she will say.

❧ Go with your friend as he undertakes the tasks of closure, including claiming the body.

❧ Remember that grief knows no timeframe, particularly when the loss is unexpected. Be patient with your friend's emotional and mental states.

❧ Assist with all the support your friend may need, as noted in previous chapters.

Redmond says in Rando's book *Treatment of Complicated Mourning,*

Homicide survivors may present symptomatic behaviors charac-teristic of post-traumatic stress disorder (PTSD) up to five years following the murder of a loved one. This becomes a normal range of functioning for this distinct population. All homicide survivors with whom I have worked were assessed at intake with some characteristics of PTSD. Survivors present with a history of nightmares, flashbacks, fear of strangers, emotional withdrawal, eating and sleeping disturbances, constant intrusion of thoughts of the murder, case-related associations, irritability, angry outbursts, and avoidance of reminders.[1]

Remember, grief over unexpected traumatic loss may last a long time. Do not expect your friend to be over the loss in a few months or even a year. We have found in our work that it generally takes twelve to eighteen months to begin to heal from such death. Be patient.

Chapter 11

Supporting Children through Grief

Children today have a familiarity with death, at least as an abstraction. They witness deaths on television, in movies, and in music. While death today is not often present in the home (as it was when it was more common for elders to die at home), children are aware of death in hospitals and of pets dying.

Discussing death with children is important, although doing so may be uncomfortable for adults. Children need to be told the truth in a straightforward manner and in a way that is age-appropriate for the child.

John's father committed suicide when John was ten years old. His mother quietly said to him, "You know that Dad has been feely very sad lately. This morning he took his life. He committed suicide." By knowing the real situation, John could work through his feelings about his dad's death. He felt free to ask questions and receive answers he could understand. Answer children's questions directly, without a great deal of detail. Children who receive accurate information do not have to imagine the worst.

You must be careful with the language you use when discussing death with children. Terms such as *asleep, passed on, passed over,* and *gone on a journey* are potentially dangerous for children who take such words literally. Imagine a child being afraid to go to sleep because *sleep* is synonymous with *death.*

A preschool teacher we know died suddenly over a weekend. A hospice children's grief counselor was asked to provide emotional support and education to the children on Monday. She stressed to the children that death was permanent, not at all like sleep. She was asked to come back the following week to help the children plant a tree in the teacher's honor. A minister was asked to offer a prayer at the ceremony. He began by saying, "Our sister who has gone to sleep with Jesus . . ." One little girl said under her breath, "No, no!"

Children grieve differently than adults. While children share the same grief emotions as adults, they often express them differently. For example, an adult may be able to express anger verbally, while a child may do so through drawing pictures. Children also grieve in spurts. One minute a child can be sad and crying in his room, and the next he's outside happily playing baseball. Children at each age grieve differently from other ages. Outlined below is how children in different age ranges view death; however, keep in mind that factors other than age influence how a child grieves. Intelligence, previous experience with death, family environment, religion, and culture also determine grief behaviors in children.

Three to Five Years Old

Children at this age often think death is reversible. Magical thinking is common. If the princess can awaken from a long sleep, so can grandfather awaken from death. It is important to tell children death is permanent, and that their loved one will not come back.

Six to Ten Years Old

By this age, children understand that death is final. They begin to realize that they, too, can die. They need to be told that just because a loved one died, they are not necessarily going to die. Children in this age range are media-savvy and are aware of murders and kidnappings committed against children. They need to be made to feel safe and protected. They need simple, honest information.

Eleven to Thirteen Years Old

Children in this age range have a realistic view of death, but refuse to believe death can happen to them. They share adult grief emotions, but often are overwhelmed by these feelings. They tend to move in and out of grief.

Teenagers

Teenagers either internalize grief or act out grief emotions in inappropriate or dangerous ways. Those who internalize grief may lead adults around them to think they are handling grief well. Look for grief emotions to sneak out, expressed in poetry, art, and music. Some children act out their grief in destructive ways, such as driving recklessly, fighting in school, experimenting with drugs and alcohol, and engaging in sexual behaviors. Regardless of how a teenager grieves, help from an adult is needed. If grief becomes pathological, seek counseling with a trained mental health professional.

Should children attend the funeral or memorial service? We believe that if a child is old enough to express his desire to attend, let him do so. Attending the service may help the child understand the finality of death, and may assist him in celebrating and mourning the death of a loved one. Explain to the child in advance of the service what he can expect to see and hear. Tell him you will be there to hold his hand.

On the contrary, if a child states that he does not want to attend, do not force him. Be sure, however, that the child has all the facts about the service, and attend to any fears the child may express. You can offer to visit the cemetery with the child later.

Cremation is often more difficult to explain to a child than burial. Keep your explanation simple. Do not use words such as *fire* and *burn,* which may frighten the child. Explain that the body was taken to a crematory where it went through a special process so that it was reduced to something that looks like sand. Mention that the ashes were put in a container called an urn, and then explain what the family plans to do with the urn.

If you are a friend to a child who is grieving, there are many ways in which you can help the child process emotions. Listed below are some things to do or not do.

What to say and do

❧ Keep routines as normal as possible.

❧ Say the deceased person's name.

❧ Talk about the person who died. Keep memories alive by looking at photos, recognizing holidays and anniversaries, and commemorating the person.

❧ Provide the child with opportunities to express feelings. These feelings may include guilt, anger, sadness, confusion, or anxiety. Listen and give your support to the idea that it is acceptable to express emotions.

❧ Be patient and adjust your behaviors to fit the child's needs.

❧ If a child becomes aggressive, try to channel his behaviors so that he understands what behaviors are acceptable, what behavioral limits are, and that he is cared for and safe.

❧ Share your feelings with the child. If you cry, explain your sadness to the child.

❧ Model appropriate grief behavior. Express your own emotions in a healthy way.

What not to say and do

❧ Avoid euphemisms such as *passed away, gone on a journey,* and *asleep.* Children take the terms literally. Be honest.

❧ Do not say, "God loved your mother so much that God sent her to heaven." A child may feel that he, too, may die if he is good.

❧ Do not say, "It was God's will." Regardless of what you as an adult believe about spirituality and death, such a statement may negatively shape a child's view of God and spirituality.

❧ Do not say, "It was best your mother died because she is no longer suffering." Perhaps a child would rather have a suffering mother than none at all.

❧ Do not say, "You're the man of the house now." The child is still a child, and should not be saddled with adult responsibilities. Also, the child cannot take the place of someone who has died.

❧ Do not say, "You must be brave." Children do not have to be brave. They should be allowed to express emotions, and to know that such expression is acceptable.

❧ Do not say, "You're doing so well" (if the child is not expressing emotion). Saying this may tell a child expression of emotions is not acceptable.

❧ Do not say, "You should be better by now." There is no timetable for grief.

❧ If a child's behavior becomes regressive, do not criticize the child. Regressive behaviors such as bed-wetting, and thumb-sucking are common after death.

As we conclude *A Good Friend for Bad Times,* we want to share with you a handout our dear friend Nan Chandler developed for adults who have grieving children:

Short Hand Rule[1]

Behavior of a grieving child and beneficial responses:
Accept
Acknowledge
Allow, when possible
Affirm
And
Act on the child's behalf

Conclusion

We hope this book is helpful to you, your friends, and your coworkers. We have shared with you acts and words of kindness that were comforting to us, our friends, and clients during our grieving process. Remember that grief is a process. For some of us, grief never ends—we simply find ways to cope with staggering losses. We urge you to be patient with your grieving friend.

Grief is individual. No two people grieve in the same way. Remember that multiple losses and old wounds contribute to how a person grieves. We do know that a strong sense of support from family, friends, and coworkers contributes to the healing process. We urge you to support your grieving friend.

Even if your friend's grief is uncomfortable for you, and even if you delay your response until some time after his loss, do call him, or at least send a card. There are no substitutes for the words, "I care about you!" We urge you to be kind, and to listen, again and again.

We believe that there is a great connectedness among us all—each of us is a part of the great gift-giving circle of life. Letting your friend know how much you care passes along the gift of the circle. Do it today.

Notes

Chapter 1

1. Granger E. Westberg, *Good Grief* (Minneapolis: Augsburg Books, 1983).
2. Elisabeth Kübler-Ross, *On Death and Dying: What the Dying Have to Teach Doctors, Nurses, Clergy, and Their Own Families* (New York: Simon & Schuster Trade Paperbacks, 1997).
3. Harold Ivan Smith, *Grievers Ask* (Minneapolis: Augsburg Books, 2004).
4. J. William Worden, *Grief Counseling and Grief Therapy: A Handbook for the Mental Health Professional* (New York: Springer Publishing Co., 2001).

Chapter 4

1. Ronald Barrett, "Affirming and Reclaiming African American Funeral Rites" in *The Director* 66, no. 11 (1994): 36-40.
2. S. B. Dowd, V. L. Poole, R. Davidhizer, and J. N. Giger, "Death, Dying and Grief in a Transcultural Context: Application of the Giger and Davidhizer Assessment Model" in *Hospice Journal* 13, no. 4 (1998): 33-56.

Chapter 6

1. Bernie S. Siegel, *Love, Medicine & Miracles: Lessons Learned about Self-Healing from a Surgeon's Experience with Exceptional Patients* (New York: HarperPerennial, 1986).
2. Denise Anderson, "I Hear You. Please Listen" in *Thanatos* 20, no. 1 (1995): 11.
3. Catherine Marshall, *Christy* (New York: McGraw Hill Book Co., 1967).

Chapter 8

1. Carl Rogers, *On Becoming a Person: A Therapist's View of Psychotherapy* (New York: Houghton Mifflin, 1995).
2. This statistic is taken from the National Institutes of Health, National Institute of Child Health and Human Development. Available from: http://www.nichd.nih.gov/womenshealth/miscarriage.cfm (retrieved 5-18-04).
3. Beryl S. Glover, *The Empty Chair: The Journey of Grief after Suicide* (Oklahoma City: In-Sight Books, Inc., 2000).
4. This statistic is taken from the WISQARS Injury Mortality Reports, 2000-2001, from the Centers for Disease Control and Prevention. Available from: http://webappa.cdc.gov/sasweb/ncipc/mortrate10_sy.html.

Chapter 10

1. L. Redmond as quoted in Theresa A. Rando, *Treatment of Complicated Mourning* (Champaign, Ill.: Research Press, 1993), 536-537.

Chapter 11

1. Nan Chandler, "Short Hand Rule." Copyright 2002 Nan Chandler. Ms. Chandler, MSW, LCSW, is Director of the Sunrise Center at Lower Cape Fear Hospice, Wilmington, North Carolina.Used with permission.

Selected Bibliography

Albom, Mitch. *Tuesdays with Morrie: An Old Man, a Young Man, and Life's Greatest Lesson.* New York: Doubleday, 1997.

Anderson, Denise. "I Hear You. Please Listen" in *Thanatos* 20, no. 1 (1995): 11.

Barrett, Ronald. "Affirming and Reclaiming African-American Funeral Rites" in *The Director* 66, no. 11 (1994): 36-40.

Bockelman, Wilfred. *Finding the Right Words: Offering Care and Comfort When You Don't Know What to Say.* Minneapolis: Augsburg Books, 1990.

Boss, Pauline. *Ambiguous Loss: Learning to Live with Unresolved Grief.* Cambridge, Mass.: Harvard University Press, 2000.

Bozarth, Alla Renee. *A Journey through Grief: Gentle, Specific Help to Get You through the Most Difficult Stages of Grieving.* Center City, Minn.: Hazelden Information & Educational Services, 1990.

Brook, Noel, and Pamela D. Blair. *I Wasn't Ready to Say Good-bye: Surviving, Coping & Healing after the Sudden Death of a Loved One.* Fox Point, Wis.: Champion Press, Ltd., 2000.

Brothers, Joyce. *Widowed.* New York: Simon & Schuster, 1990.

Burke, Theresa, and David C. Reardon. *Forbidden Grief: The Unspoken Pain of Abortion.* Kansas City, Mo.: Acorn Books, 2002.

Callanan, Maggie, and Patricia D. Kelley. *Final Gifts: Understanding the Special Awareness, Needs and Communications of the Dying.* New York: Bantam Books, 1997.

Chethik, Neil. *Father Loss: How Sons of All Ages Come to Terms with the Deaths of Their Dads.* New York: Hyperion, 2001.

Dodd, Robert V. *When Someone You Love Dies: An Explanation of Death for Children.* Nashville: Abingdon Press, 1989.

Donnelly, Katherine F. *Recovering from the Loss of a Parent.* New York: Berkley Publishing Group, 1994.

Dowd, S. B., V. L. Poole, R. Davidhizer, and J. N. Giger. "Death, Dying and Grief in a Transcultural Context: Application of the Giger and Davidhizer Assessment Model" in *Hospice Journal* 13, no. 4 (1998): 33-56.

Dower, Laura. *I Will Remember You: What to Do When Someone You Love Dies: A Guidebook through Grief for Teens.* New York: Scholastic, Inc., 2000.

Edelman, Hope, ed., *Letters from Motherless Daughters: Words of Courage, Grief and Healing.* New York: Dell Publishing, 1996.

Exupery, Antonie de Saint. *The Little Prince.* New York: Harcourt Brace Jovanorich, Inc. 1943.

Fitzgerald, Helen. *The Grieving Child: A Parent's Guide.* New York: Simon & Schuster. 1992.

———. *The Mourning Handbook: The Most Comprehensive Resource Offering Practical and Compassionate Advice on Coping with All Aspects of Death and Dying.* New York: Simon & Schuster, 1994.

Glover, Beryl S. *The Empty Chair: The Journey of Grief after Suicide.* Oklahoma City: In-Sight Books, Inc., 2000.

Grollman, Earl A. *Straight Talk about Death for Teenagers.* Boston: Beacon, 1993.

Guthrie, Nancy. *Holding on to Hope: Drawn by Suffering to the Heart of God.* Carol Stream, Ill.: Tyndale House Publishing, 2002.

Hickman, Martha Whitmore. *Healing after Loss: Daily Meditations for Working through Grief.* New York: Morrow, William & Co., 1994.

Huntley, Theresa. *Helping Children Grieve When Someone They Love Dies.* Minneapolis: Augsburg Books, 2002.

Ilse, Sherokee, ed., *Empty Arms: Coping after Miscarriage, Stillbirth and Infant Death.* Maple Plain, Mich.: Wintergreen Press, 2002.

James, John W., and Russell Friedman. *The Grief Recovery Handbook: The Action Program for Moving Beyond Death, Divorce and Other Losses*. New York: Harper-Collins, 1998.

Jensen, Amy Hillyard. *Healing Grief,* 2nd ed. Redmond, Wash.: Medic Publishing Co., 1995.

Kübler-Ross, Elisabeth. *Death: The Final Stage of Growth*. Englewood Cliffs, N.J.: Prentice-Hall, Inc., 1975.

———. *On Death and Dying: What the Dying Have to Teach Doctors, Nurses, Clergy and Their Own Families*. New York: Simon & Schuster Trade Paperbacks, 1997.

———. *To Live until We Say Good-bye*. New York: Simon & Schuster Trade Paperbacks, 2000.

———. *Working It Through: An Elisabeth Kübler-Ross Workshop on Life, Death and Transition*. New York: Simon & Schuster, 1997.

Levy, Alexander. *The Orphaned Adult: Understanding and Coping with Grief and Change after the Death of Our Parents*. Cambridge, Mass.: Perseus Publishing, 2000.

Lewis, C. S. *A Grief Observed*. San Francisco: HarperSanFrancisco, 2001.

Marshall, Catherine. *Christy*. New York: McGraw Hill Book Co., 1967.

Peterson, Kathrine, Fannie R. Palmer, and Trisha Smith. *Write from Your Heart: A Healing Grief Journal*. South Berwick, Maine: Garrison Oaks Publishing, 2001.

Rando, Theresa A. *Grief, Dying and Death: Clinical Interventions for Caregivers*. Champaign, Ill.: Research Press, 1984.

———. *Treatment of Complicated Mourning*. Champaign, Ill.: Research Press, 1993, 536-537.

Ray, M. Catherine. *I'm Here to Help: A Hospice Worker's Guide to Communicating with Dying People and Their Loved Ones*. Mound, Minn.: Hospice Handouts, a Division of McRay Co., 1992.

Rogers, Carl. *On Becoming a Person: A Therapist's View of Psychotherapy*. New York: Houghton Mifflin, 1995.

Siegel, Bernie S. *Love, Medicine and Miracles: Lessons Learned about Self-Healing from a Surgeon's Experience with Exceptional Patients*. New York: HarperPerennial, 1986.

Silverstein, Shel. *The Giving Tree*. New York: Harper Collins Children's Books, 1964.

Smith, Harold Ivan. *Grievers Ask*. Minneapolis: Augsburg Books, 2004.

———. *Grieving the Death of a Friend.* Minneapolis: Augsburg Books, 1996.

———. *Grieving the Death of a Mother.* Minneapolis: Augsburg Books, 2003.

———. *On Grieving the Death of a Father.* Minneapolis: Augsburg Books, 1994.

Sogyal, Rinpoche S., P. D. Gaffney, and A. Harvey. *The Tibetan Book of Living and Dying: The Spiritual Classic and International Bestseller,* rev. ed. San Francisco: HarperSanFrancisco, 1994.

Staudacher, Carol. *Beyond Grief: A Guide to Recovering from the Death of a Loved One.* Oakland, Calif.: New Harbinger Publications, Inc. 1987.

———. *Men and Grief.* Oakland, Calif.: New Harbinger Publications, Inc. 1991.

Stuparyk, Emily Margaret. *When Only the Love Remains: The Pain of Pet Loss.* Toronto, Ontario: Hushion House, 2000.

Tatelbaum, Judy. *The Courage to Grieve.* New York: Harper & Row Publishers, 1980.

VanPraagh, James. *Healing Grief: Reclaiming Life after Any Loss.* New York: Penguin Audio Books, 2000.

Westberg, Granger E. *Good Grief.* Minneapolis: Augsburg Books, 1983.

White, E. B. *Charlotte's Web.* New York: Harper & Row, 1952.

Williams, Margery. *The Velveteen Rabbit.* New York: Doubleday & Co., 1986.

Worden, J. William. *Children and Grief: When a Parent Dies.* New York: Guilford Press, 1996.

———. *Grief Counseling and Grief Therapy: A Handbook for the Mental Health Professional.* New York: Springer Publishing Co., 2001.

Zonnebelt-Smeenge, Susan J., and Robert DeVries. *Getting to the Other Side of Grief: Overcoming the Loss of a Spouse.* Grand Rapids: Baker Book House, 1998.

Internet Resources

Administration on Aging: aoa.dhhs.gov
Aging with Dignity: agingwithdignity.org
American Academy of Hospice and Palliative Medicine:
    aahpm.org
American Association of Retired Persons: aarp.org
American Health Decisions: ahd.org
American Hospice Foundation: americanhospice.org
American Pain Society: ampainsoc.org
Americans for Better Care of the Dying: abcd-caring.org
Caregiver.com: caregiver.com
Compassionate Friends: compassionatefriends.org
Death and Dying Grief Support: death-dying.com
Dying Well: dyingwell.org
Hospice Foundation of America: hospicefoundation.org
Last Acts: Campaigning to Improve End-of-Life Care:
    lastacts.org
National Family Caregivers Association: nfcacares.org

On Our Own Terms: Moyers on Dying in America:
   pbs.org/onourownterms
Project on Death in America: soros.org/death
Rites of Passage: ktc.net/ritesofpassage

*Web sites were current as of May 2004, but may not always be
   up to date.

About the Authors

Deborah E. Bowen, MSW, LCSW, is a clinical social worker in Wrightsville Beach, North Carolina. She has been in private practice since 1993. Deb specializes in grief counseling, counseling the elderly and terminally ill, and counseling their caregivers. She is a lecturer in the department of social work at the University of North Carolina at Wilmington, and is a former lecturer in the Graduate School at East Carolina University's School of Social Work. She holds a Bachelor of Arts in psychology and a Master of Social Work with an emphasis on health and aging. Deb is a member of the National Association of Social Workers, and is a member of NASW-NC's board of directors. She is an article reviewer for the journal *Health Care for Women International*. She is trained as a facilitator in the Gundersen Lutheran Medical Foundation's Respecting Choices™ Advance Care Planning program. She is a consultant and mental health practitioner for disaster agencies, and frequently lectures to professionals and lay people on caregiver and grief issues. Before receiving her MSW,

Deb was a technical writer for eleven years, authoring numerous text- and audio-based training programs. For fun, Deb gardens, takes students on service trips, acts in local theater productions, and hosts a radio program, *The Magnolia Fatback Folk Hour*, on Public Radio station WHQR.

Susan Lamson Strickler, MEd, has worked as a bereavement counselor at Lower Cape Fear Hospice and LifeCareCenter, Inc., Wilmington, North Carolina, since 1991 and has coordinated the agency's bereavement programs since 1997. She provides both individual and group counseling for hospice families and the community at large. Sue has developed several specialized group counseling programs including Adults Who Have Had a Parent Die, Living with Grief, and Loss and the Holidays. Sue holds a Bachelor of Arts in sociology and education and a Master of Education with an emphasis in geriatrics. She is a member of the American Counseling Association, the Association for Death Education and Counseling, and the American Association of University Women. Through her church, she is a Stephen Minister and Leader.